Research Methods in
PSYCHOLOGY

Student Lab Guide

Carrie Cuttler

University of British Columbia

Kendall Hunt
publishing company

Cover images © 2010, Shutterstock Inc.

Kendall Hunt
publishing company

www.kendallhunt.com
Send all inquiries to:
4050 Westmark Drive
Dubuque, IA 52004-1840

Copyright © 2010 by Kendall Hunt Publishing Company

ISBN 978-0-7575-7968-4

Printed in the United States of America
10 9 8 7 6 5 4 3

Contents

Introduction and Overview

The purpose of the labs detailed in this guide is to give you hands-on experience with every stage of the research process. The development and growth of knowledge depends on research. The various types of designs that you will learn about in your research methods course are invaluable tools that researchers in psychology require to put together the pieces of the human puzzle. The following labs were developed to complement the lecture and textbook components of your research methods course: specifically, they were designed to provide you with the opportunity to directly apply the knowledge you gain from your course. Decades of memory research have established that active engagement with material promotes deeper and longer-term learning. Participation in the labs will provide you with a deeper understanding of the core concepts you learn about in the classroom and will give you the foundation and experience necessary to conduct and critically evaluate others' research.

For the labs, you will be working with a research team containing a few of your peers. During the first lab meeting, you will meet with your research team to brainstorm a research question and to design a simple study. For the second meeting, each research team will give a brief presentation proposing their study. Following each presentation, the class will discuss the strengths and limitations of the proposed study and will provide feedback to strengthen its design. In the third lab meeting, you will have the opportunity to conduct your study, using your classmates as participants, as well as to participate in other teams' studies. In the fourth lab, you will learn how to summarize and present your data in a meaningful way. Finally, in the fifth lab, you will learn how to write a research report using the style of the American Psychological Association (APA).

Enter the designated dates and locations for each lab meeting in the space provided below.

Lab Overview	Lab Dates	Lab Meeting Room
Lab 1: Brainstorming		
Lab 2: Proposal		
Lab 3: Data Collection		
Lab 4: Data Summary		
Lab 5: Writing an APA Style Research Report		

Enter the names and contact information of the members of your research team in the space below.

My Research Team	Contact Information

Advice on Group Work

You will be expected to complete the labs with a small group of your peers (in small research teams). This is not only for practical reasons, but also because research is rarely conducted in isolation and teamwork is typically required of researchers. Working in a team (especially a team of individuals you do not know well) can be challenging. The following advice is intended to minimize these challenges.

1. Be respectful of each other. Try not to interrupt your team members while they are talking and be careful not to dominate the discussion. Be sure to acknowledge others' ideas and to consider their merits before outright rejecting them. Rather than simply dismissing something as a "bad idea," politely explain the potential problems with the idea using positive language.

2. Stay actively involved in the process. Be sure to provide input and ask questions. Do not sit back and allow others to do the work for you. Not only can this create resentment, it will also limit your ability to produce a quality research report.

3. Make sure it is clear who is going to be responsible for completing various tasks and ensure that each team member has a deadline to complete their assigned tasks (this deadline should never be the next lab meeting date). Be sure to follow through with your commitments and agreements to have tasks completed on time. Teams are encouraged to designate a task manager to be responsible for checking up on team members and ensuring people are staying on track. If you become severely ill or have an emergency that will prevent you from completing a task or attending a lab meeting, contact your teammates immediately to inform them. For this reason, it is a good idea to exchange emergency contact information.

4. Stay in communication with your team. It will be necessary for you to meet with your team outside of the lab meeting days/times to prepare for the proposal, to prepare the materials for your study, to practice conducting your study in a consistent manner, and to share the data. You will need to do your best to make yourself available for these extra meetings and to contribute to work that needs to be done outside of class time.

5. Stay on task and complete your work efficiently. Produce the highest quality work possible. Remember your team is depending on you.

BRAINSTORMING

Objectives

- To brainstorm a research question
- To design a brief study to address your research question

By the end of the first lab meeting, your research team is expected to arrive at a research question and to design a brief study to address the question. Keep your research question and design simple and concise. Examples of appropriate research questions and designs are provided in Appendix 1. Creativity is certainly encouraged, but keep in mind that the *process* of conducting the research matters more than your specific topic.

© Bruce Rolf, 2010. Used under license from Shutterstock, Inc.

Advanced Preparation

Before meeting with your research team for the first lab, you should complete the following four tasks:

- ❏ Carefully review the information in this guide pertaining to the first and second labs.
- ❏ Complete the Tri-Council Policy Statement (TCPS) ethics tutorial and print your certificate.
- ❏ Brainstorm your own research question.
- ❏ Brainstorm a design to address your research question.

Information on the TCPS ethics tutorial and information to assist you in brainstorming a research question and design are provided below. You should review the information below, complete the tasks listed above, and check the box next to each task to indicate its completion. You will be prepared for the first lab once all four boxes are checked. Note that Appendix 1 contains examples of appropriate research questions and designs, which you also may wish to review.

Ethical Considerations

In 1998, the three leading Canadian federal research funding agencies teamed together to create the Tri-Council Policy Statement (TCPS), a document outlining various ethical considerations and the obligations of researchers conducting research with human participants. Since you will be using your fellow classmates as participants in your study, you need to familiarize yourself with this code of ethics and complete and pass the TCPS ethics tutorial before the first lab. The tutorial takes about two hours to complete and can be found at http://www.pre.ethics.gc.ca/english/tutorial/ ?action=start. After successfully completing the tutorial, you will receive a certificate of completion, which you can print and turn in to your instructor before the first lab.

Be sure to pay special attention to the section of the tutorial discussing minimal risk research, as the study you conduct will need to be classified as minimal risk in order for you to be permitted to execute it in the third lab. According to the TCPS, research is considered minimal risk if it entails no greater probability and magnitude of possible harms than those encountered by the subject in aspects of his or her everyday life. Thus, participants in your study must not be required to perform tasks that have the potential to cause any psychological or physical discomfort. You may ask participants to answer general questions, to answer personal questions of a non-invasive nature, and/or to perform everyday tasks (e.g., puzzles, reading, simple non-invasive tests). You may NOT collect any private or sensitive information (e.g., information on drug use, sexual habits, income, etc.). If you use headphones, drinking cups, or similar materials, you must make sure to properly sanitize them between subjects (ideally, disposable materials should be used).

Brainstorming a Research Question

Developing a research question can be time-consuming and difficult. Thus, it is important that you start the brainstorming process early. Ideally, you should begin brainstorming research questions before meeting with your group for the first time. The following is intended to guide you through the brainstorming process.

Start by considering which area of psychology interests you the most. For instance, are you interested in cognitive psychology, social psychology, forensic psychology, clinical psychology, developmental psychology, health psychology, or industrial organization psychology? Keep in mind, some areas will be more difficult to address given the practical limitations of the labs. For instance, it may be more difficult to arrive at a research question pertaining to clinical psychology or forensic psychology because you will be limited to using your classmates as participants and to minimal risk research designs (see Study Checklist on page 8).

Area(s) of Interest

Use the space provided below to identify the area(s) of psychology you are interested in researching.

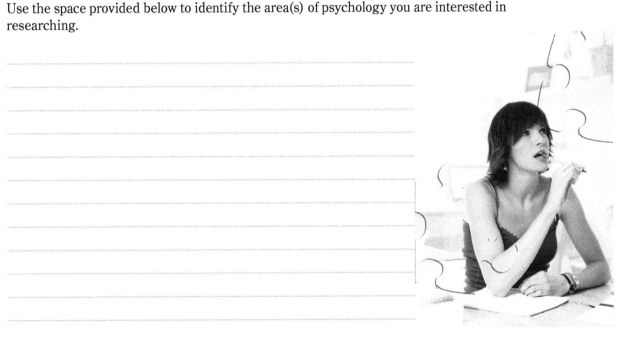

© Jan Martin Will, 2010. Used under license from Shutterstock, Inc.

Once you have identified an area of psychology that you are interested in exploring, you can begin trying to narrow things down a little by considering topics/issues that are commonly addressed in the area. For instance, topics addressed in cognitive psychology include memory, attention, perception, sensation, decision making, and reasoning. Issues addressed in social psychology include conformity, stereotypes, belief formation, helping behaviour, and personality. Industrial organization psychology focuses on work-related factors such as motivation, productivity, effective management, and personnel selection. A simple online search of the area of psychology that interests you most may help you to narrow down the area to one or two topics or issues that you would like to pursue. Alternatively, you may consider some of the studies you learned about in your psychology classes and think about ways in which you could follow up on one.

Topics/Issues of Interest

Use the space provided below to identify the topics/issues you are interested in researching.

Next, you should begin thinking about specific variables that you could manipulate and measure. For instance, if you decided you are interested in memory, start thinking about variables that may affect memory (e.g., distraction). If you decided you are interested in motivation, try to brainstorm variables that may affect people's motivation (e.g., exposure to a success story). You will likely be able to come up with a more creative and original idea using your own intuition, insights, and experience, rather than relying on reading the literature at this point.

Variables of Interest

Use the space provided below to identify variables you are interested in manipulating and measuring.

Once you have further refined your thinking to specific variables you can manipulate and measure, you should start looking for previous related research to read and review. You should use your library's PsycInfo database to find articles related to your variables of interest. After reading previous articles on the topic, you may be able to further refine your idea and/or discover important methodological considerations. It will also give you a jump-start on your research report, as you will need to provide some discussion of previous related research in your report.

Related Articles

Use the space below to identify previously published articles and to note important considerations.

After you have had a chance to familiarize yourself with previous research on your topic of interest, you can begin to try to develop specific research questions. Remember to keep your question simple and concise. Also, consider whether you will be able to address the question using a simple minimal risk study that can be conducted on your classmates in a busy classroom environment (see Study Checklist on page 8).

Potential Research Questions

Use the space below to record specific research questions you would be interested in addressing.

Selecting an Appropriate Research Design

The following is intended to provide a brief summary of some commonly used experimental and non-experimental research designs, as well as some of the strengths and limitations associated with each. The information provided below is not intended to be an exhaustive list of all designs, strengths, and limitations and should be used in conjunction with your research methods textbook and lecture notes to assist you in identifying a design appropriate to address your research question.

Experimental Designs

Posttest Only Design

An independent variable is manipulated to create two or more groups/conditions while all other variables are held constant across the groups/conditions. The independent variable's effect on the dependent variable is measured by comparing the levels of the dependent variable across the groups/conditions.

> Considerations: Method of assignment of participants to groups—independent groups or repeated measures (see boxes below for strengths and limitations associated with each).
>
> Strengths: Permits determination of causation and is simple and straightforward.
>
> Limitations: Vary depending on whether independent groups or repeated measures design is used in conjunction with the design (see boxes below).

Independent Groups	
Different people are randomly assigned to participate in the different groups.	

Group 1	Group 2
Sally	John
Mark	Jason
Tim	Amy

Strengths: Counterbalancing is not required because order effects are not of concern.

Limitations: Random assignment may not produce equivalent independent groups when only small samples can be obtained, so the people in the various groups may have preexisting differences.

Repeated Measures	
The same people participate in the different conditions.	

Group 1	Group 2
Sally	Sally
Mark	Mark
Tim	Tim

Strengths: Reduces random variability and allows you to ensure that the people in the various conditions do not have preexisting differences without the use of a pretest.

Limitations: Requires the use of counterbalancing to control for potential order effects.

Pretest-Posttest Design

A pretest of the dependent variable is first administered. An independent variable is then manipulated to create two or more independent groups while all other variables are held constant across the groups. The independent variable's effect on the dependent variable is measured by comparing the levels of the dependent variable across the groups.

Ceiling Effect: All participants perform near the maximum performance level (i.e., perfectly or near perfectly) on the dependent variable, rendering it difficult to detect differences across groups/conditions.

Strengths: Permits determination of causation and allows you to confirm that people in the independent groups did not have any preexisting differences with respect to the dependent variable.

Limitations: More time-consuming. Pretest may serve as a demand characteristic or otherwise influence the final measure of the dependent variable.

Non-Experimental Designs

Non-Equivalent Control Group Design

An independent variable is not manipulated: rather, the levels of the dependent variable are simply compared across preexisting groups of people (e.g., males vs. females).

Strengths: Useful when the variable of interest cannot be manipulated for ethical or practical reasons.

Limitations: Causation cannot be determined due to potential selection biases (i.e., other preexisting differences across the groups may account for differences in the levels of the dependent variable).

Correlational Design

Two variables are simply measured and the direction and degree to which they are associated is examined. Nothing is manipulated and no groups of participants are formed.

Strengths: Useful for describing relationships and for making predictions. Useful when the variables of interest cannot be manipulated for ethical or practical reasons.

Limitations: Causation cannot be determined due to the third variable and directionality problems. Somewhat less intuitive analysis required.

Floor Effect: All participants perform near the minimum performance level on the dependent variable, rendering it difficult to detect differences across the groups/conditions.

Study Checklist

Your study must have the following properties. Carefully review each property with your research team and check the box next to each to indicate that your study meets the criteria.

❏ **Minimal Risk:** Your study must be minimal risk. According to the TCPS, research is considered minimal risk if it entails no greater probability and magnitude of possible harms than those encountered by the subject in aspects of his or her everyday life. You may NOT request private or sensitive information (e.g., information on drug use, sexual habits, income, etc.), and studies must not entail any possibility of physical or psychological harm. If you use headphones, drinking cups, or similar materials, you must use disposable materials or properly sanitize them between subjects.

❏ **Practical:** Your study must be designed such that it can be conducted in a busy classroom environment. Collecting any data outside of the designated time or from anyone other than your classmates, instructor, and teaching assistants is prohibited for ethical reasons.

❏ **Brief:** To ensure that everyone has time to participate in the other teams' studies and to ensure that you are able to collect a sufficient amount of data (i.e., at least 10 participants in total), your study must be designed such that each participant can complete it in 5 minutes or less. Keep in mind that you will be able to collect data from more subjects if you require less time of them and if you can test more than one participant at a time.

❏ **Feasible:** You must be able to obtain or create all of the materials necessary to conduct your study before the third lab.

Lab 1 worksheet

By the end of the first lab, you should be able to answer each of the following questions. Use the space below to fill in your answers.

1. What is your research question?

2. What type of design will you use to address your question?

3. Describe your method. Specifically, what will participants have to do?

4. What is your independent variable?

    a. How do you plan to manipulate it?

5. What is your dependent variable?

    a. How do you plan to measure it?

6. Are there any controls you plan to implement?

7. What is your hypothesis?

During the next lab meeting, your research team will be required to propose your research question and design to your class via a brief (5 minute) oral presentation. Before this time, your team will need to create and rehearse your presentation. Use this worksheet to identify who will be responsible for completing each of the following tasks and the date by which each should be completed. More than one team member should be responsible for each duty, and all group members should be given a chance to contribute and provide input on each of the various tasks. The group due date should represent the date the task should be completed and submitted to the research team for evaluation, comments, and further refinement. The class due date should be the date the instructor has assigned for your team to deliver your proposal.

This worksheet is intended to help you form a contract with your group. Members should sign their names under the tasks for which they volunteer to acknowledge their responsibility for completing those tasks on or before the group due date identified.

Names and Signatures of Members Responsible for Creating Presentation Outline:

Group Due Date:

Names and Signatures of Members Responsible for Creating PowerPoint Presentation:

Group Due Date:

Names and Signatures of Members Responsible for Rehearsing and Delivering Presentation:

Group Due Date (Rehearsal):   **Class Due Date (Final Delivery):**

PROPOSAL

Objectives

- To propose your research question and design to your class
- To elicit feedback from your class to improve your design
- To provide feedback and input on other groups' designs

During the second lab meeting, your research team will be expected to give a brief (5 min) presentation of your proposed research question and design. Each presentation will be followed by a brief discussion period where your classmates, teaching assistant, and instructor will ask questions and provide suggestions for improvement. Following other research teams' proposal presentations, you will be expected to provide input and feedback on their designs.

© zhu difeng, 2010. Used under license from Shutterstock, Inc.

Advanced Preparation

Before the second lab meeting, you and your team will need to complete the following five tasks:

- ❏ Carefully review the information in this guide pertaining to the second and third labs.
- ❏ Outline the major points you want to make in your proposal presentation.
- ❏ Create your presentation using PowerPoint or comparable presentation software.
- ❏ Practice giving your presentation both on your own and as a team.
- ❏ Prepare to give some peer review after other teams' proposals.

Information to assist you in developing your proposal presentation and to help you prepare for the peer review process is provided below. You should review the information below, complete the tasks listed above, and check the box next to each task to indicate its completion. You will be prepared for the second lab once all five boxes are checked.

Presentation Outline

Your proposal presentation should address the following points. Use the space provided on this worksheet to outline the specific information you will provide for each.

Presentation Outline Worksheet

1. Introduce your research topic.

   a. You may wish to provide a real world context to introduce your research question.

   b. State your research question.

   c. Sell your idea.

      i. Provide information on why your question is interesting, important, and/or relevant.

      ii. You may wish to briefly discuss some previous related research that inspired or guided the development of your research question.

2. Clearly describe the design and procedure you will use. In doing so, be sure to:

   a. Identify the type of design you plan to use.

   b. Identify the independent variable and how it will be manipulated.

   c. Identify the dependent variable and how it will be measured.

   d. You may also choose to demonstrate some of the materials you will use.

   e. If relevant, identify whether you will use an independent groups or repeated measures design and provide some justification for this decision.

   f. If relevant, discuss any controls you plan to implement to ensure there are no confounds in your experiment.

3. Explain your hypothesis.

   a. Describe what outcome you expect for your project (i.e., what you expect to find).

   b. You may also wish to describe the implications of such findings.

Presentation Tips

You will need to consult with your instructor and/or teaching assistant to determine whether the presentation must be delivered as a group or whether you are permitted to nominate a spokesperson to deliver the entire presentation. If the presentation is to be completed as a group, you should break it into sections and assign a different member of your team to each section. If a spokesperson will be nominated, then the individuals who are not involved in giving the presentation should make an extra effort in preparing the presentation and/or study materials.

You are encouraged to use PowerPoint or comparable presentation software to prepare and deliver your proposal. PowerPoint will make your presentation appear more professional and polished. If, like many people, you tend to have a difficult time remembering what you need to say when you are nervous, the information on the PowerPoint slides can help you stay on point while avoiding the need to rely on notes. Slides also provide a visual aid for your audience, meaning they are not just staring at you! Clip art and illustrations should be used to keep your audience engaged. In developing your presentation, you should try to keep the information on the slides at a minimum. The slides should only be used as a visual aid; it is up to you to convey the information in a clear, concise manner.

When delivering your presentation, be sure to speak in a loud, clear, confident voice. Try to vary your pitch and tone so you don't sound monotone. Also, try not to stand like you are glued to one spot on the floor. Move around a little bit during your presentation, use hand gestures where appropriate, and most importantly, be enthusiastic! After all, if you do not seem interested in the information you are presenting, then it will be difficult to get anyone else interested.

Following your team's presentation, you will need to elicit feedback from your peers and attempt to answer any questions they may have. It is common for people to feel threatened and to behave defensively when a flaw in their project is pointed out or when they are asked a challenging question. Try to keep in mind that the role of your peers is to support you and to help you to improve your study. Rather than reacting to a perceived criticism defensively, you should aim to show your appreciation for the advice and politely explain why you do or do not share the opinion expressed. For instance, if you chose to use a repeated measures design and someone challenges this decision, you may begin by identifying your knowledge of the limitations of this design and then proceed to discuss your reasons for opting to use this design (i.e., why you feel the strengths outweigh the limitations). If you display defensiveness or hostility, your peers will be less likely to provide their input and important considerations may not be voiced, ultimately undermining the integrity of your research study.

When responding to more complex questions, it is good form to first acknowledge the question by either rephrasing the question yourself (this helps to ensure that you properly understand the question, and therefore, that you answer the correct question) or commenting that the question is interesting. If you are asked a particularly challenging question that you don't know how to answer, you should politely ask the individual to rephrase or further explain the question. If you still do not understand the question after it is rephrased, or if you do not know how to answer the question, you should feel free to turn to your research team for their thoughts and input. You are not expected to know everything. Sometimes it is sufficient to simply respond to a question by indicating that you have not formerly considered the

© RTimages, 2010. Used under license from Shutterstock, Inc.

issue, giving assurance that your research team will consider or discuss it together at a later time, and thanking the individual for his/her thought-provoking insights.

If you are not used to presenting in front of a group of people, it is a good idea to practice in front of a mirror or videotape yourself so you can observe your facial expressions and body language while delivering your presentation. Many people have unconscious habits (e.g., saying "um" very frequently, looking down, fidgeting, talking very rapidly) that can be distracting during a presentation. The best way to become aware of any unconscious habits you may have is to watch yourself giving your presentation. You may think you look and sound professional during your practice sessions, but the image of yourself that you see in the mirror or video may indicate otherwise. Watching yourself give a presentation is not a very comfortable experience, but it can provide invaluable feedback, allowing you to discover and correct your distracting habits before displaying them in front of a group of your peers.

Peer Review

Science is a public enterprise. As such, peer review is an essential component of the research process. Before a research team is given money by a granting agency or foundation, they must submit a proposal that is critically reviewed, evaluated, and ranked by a panel of experts. Only those with the highest quality proposals are given the funds to execute their project. In addition, before researchers are given the opportunity to disseminate their research findings at a conference or in a professional journal, the research they wish to publish undergoes a process of peer review. In the case of a journal publication, a journal editor distributes copies of the research report to two or more experts in the area of research. The experts critically evaluate the report and the research described within, and then each reviewer sends his/her comments to the journal editor, who renders a final decision. The editor may decide that the research is ready for publication, that it requires more work before being ready for publication, or that it is simply unacceptable for publication.

Since peer review is such an integral component of the research process, you will be expected to engage in some peer review after each team's proposal presentation. You should help each team to identify possible confounds and design issues and/or provide

suggestions on how teams can improve their research projects. In order to be a competent and constructive reviewer, you will need to have a solid understanding of the basic experimental and non-experimental designs and the various design issues that researchers need to consider. As such, you should be sure to review your lecture notes and the relevant chapters of your textbook before the lab. Research shows that one of the most effective ways of learning is by teaching and helping others. If you use this peer review process as an opportunity to apply what you have learned in the classroom and from the textbook, you will find that you will develop a deeper understanding of the material than you thought possible.

While listening to each proposal, you should consider some of the following questions, as they may be useful in helping you to provide each team with constructive feedback and advice. A few blank points have been included for you to add your own questions after you have reviewed your text and notes.

1. Do you agree with the decision to use an independent groups/repeated measures design? What are the pros and cons of each for this particular study?

2. Are there any potential confounds? How could they be controlled?

3. Are there potential floor and/or ceiling effects? How can they be resolved?

4. Are there any ethical concerns? What steps could be taken to make the procedure more ethical?

5. Are there any practical problems? Can the study be conducted in a busy classroom?

6. Is the study feasible? Will the group be able to collect/create the materials by the designated date for data collection?

7.

8.

9.

10.

Lab 2 worksheet

You should answer each of the following questions after the second lab. Use the space below to fill in your answers.

1. Provide a brief summary of the feedback your team obtained. What changes were suggested?

2. Which of those suggested changes do you plan to make and how will you implement each?

3. Which of those suggested changes do you plan to ignore?

    a. Provide a brief explanation for why you have chosen to ignore those suggested changes.

Division of Duties

You will need to be ready to collect data for your study during the next lab meeting, as it will be your one and only opportunity to do so. Use the following worksheet to list all of the various materials you will require to conduct your study and to identify which team members will be responsible for collecting or creating each. Identify a group due date, which should represent the date the materials should be completed and submitted to the group for evaluation, comments, and further refinement. Second, identify the class due date, which should represent the date the instructor has designated for data collection. Be sure to leave enough time between the group due date and the class due date for your team to meet to review the materials and pilot test the study. Since you will be given only one opportunity to collect data, you should ensure that all materials are compiled well before the next lab meeting and that you have backup plans in place in case of a team member's unexpected absence.

This worksheet is intended to help you form a contract with your group. List all of the materials that you will need to conduct your study, and ask members to sign their names next to those they volunteer to collect/create, to acknowledge their responsibility for doing so on or before the group due date identified. Instead of dividing up the duties to create the various materials, you may wish to meet to work together as a team to create the necessary materials.

Use the space provided below to list all required materials, along with the names and signatures of those responsible for collecting/creating each:

Required Materials	Team Member(s) Responsible

Group Due Date:

Class Due Date:

DATA COLLECTION

Objectives

- To collect data for your team's study
- To participate in all other research teams' studies

The third lab meeting will be the ONLY opportunity for your research team to collect data. Collecting data outside this lab meeting time or with individuals other than your classmates, teaching assistants, and instructor is strictly prohibited for ethical reasons and may result in major deductions to your team's project.

© Pixel 4 Images, 2010. Used under license from Shutterstock, Inc.

Advanced Preparation

Before the third lab meeting, your research team should complete the following five tasks:

- ❏ Carefully review this chapter of the guide.
- ❏ Collect, create, and compile all of the materials necessary to conduct your study.
- ❏ Review the materials as a team and make any necessary adjustments.
- ❏ Pilot test your study as a team and make any necessary changes.
- ❏ Rehearse your role as experimenter with your team and on your own.

Information to assist you in pilot testing your study is provided below. After completing each of the tasks listed above, check the corresponding box to indicate its completion. You will be prepared for the third lab once all five boxes are checked.

Lab Expectations

This lab meeting will be your team's only opportunity to collect data for your study. During the lab meeting time, you will be expected to take turns with your team members playing the role of the experimenter (collecting data for your research team's study) and participant (participating in all other research teams' studies). Each member of your team should test at least two participants, and together your team should aim to collect data from at least 10 participants in total. To ensure that all research teams collect enough data for their studies, a maximum of two experimenters should test participants in your study at any given moment while your remaining team members participate in other groups' studies. Each study will be minimal risk, but you have the right to refuse to participate in any study (or respond to specific questions or perform certain tasks) that makes you feel uncomfortable.

Pilot Testing

Before arriving at the third lab meeting, your team should meet to compile and review all of the materials that you will use in your study and make any necessary adjustments to them. You will also need to make sure that your team has a well rehearsed standardized procedure to follow. To fulfill the lab expectations (described above), you should make sure that your procedure requires a maximum of two experimenters to conduct. Since each team member will be expected to spend some time as an experimenter, it is a good idea to create a short script for experimenters to follow. Creating a script together will help your team ensure that everyone is comfortable in the role of the experimenter and that the study is conducted in a consistent fashion across experimenters.

Once all of the team members are comfortable with the procedure/script, you should work together to pilot test your study. A pilot test is essentially a dry run of the study. It provides an opportunity for researchers to practice conducting their study and to identify any potential problems with it. As such, it is always a good idea to pilot test a study before beginning to collect data. It is particularly important for your team to conduct some pilot testing because you will only have one opportunity to collect your data. Data collection day is not the time you want to find problems with your procedure! Since the experimenter and participant often perceive the study in very different ways, and to give everyone a chance to practice playing both roles, team members should take turns playing the roles of experimenter and participant during the pilot testing.

Pilot Testing worksheet

To make sure you are ready to conduct your study, during the pilot testing you should answer each of the following questions:

❏ Do you have all of the materials necessary to conduct the study and record the data?
Yes ☐   No ☐
○ If no, what additional materials are necessary, who will produce them, and when will they complete them and submit them to the group?

❏ Does it take 5 minutes or less to run one participant through the study from start to finish?
Yes ☐   No ☐
○ If no, what changes will be made to shorten the study? Who will be responsible for making these changes and when will they be completed and submitted to the group?

❏ Did you identify any demand characteristics?
Yes ☐   No ☐
○ If yes, what changes can be made to eliminate or reduce the demand characteristics? Who will be responsible for making these changes and when will they be completed and submitted to the group? Note that demand characteristics should not be a major concern for your purposes, especially since your hypothesis was already described to potential participants during your proposal presentation.

❏ Did you identify any confounds?

Yes ☐   No ☐

○ If yes, what changes can be made to the study to eliminate the confound(s)? Who will be responsible for making these changes and when will they be completed and submitted to the group?

❏ Are the tasks too easy or too hard? Is there a chance you will end up with ceiling or floor effects?

Yes ☐   No ☐

○ If yes, what changes can be made to increase/decrease the difficulty level of the tasks? Who will be responsible for making the changes and when will they be completed and submitted to the group?

❏ Are any additional changes necessary?

Yes ☐   No ☐

○ If yes, describe the changes necessary. Who will be responsible for making these changes and when will they be completed and submitted to the group?

❏ Are all of the experimenters comfortable in their role?

Yes ☐   No ☐

❏ Are all of the experimenters conducting the study in a consistent fashion?

Yes ☐   No ☐

Create a Backup Plan

Researchers sometimes only have a rare, one-time opportunity to collect data for their studies. This is especially common when researchers must get special permission to conduct their studies in institutions other than their home university. For instance, forensic psychologists often need to make special arrangements with penitentiaries to test prisoners in their studies, clinical psychologists often need to get permission from hospitals to collect data from patients, and developmental psychologists are occasionally invited to schools to conduct research with students. In each of these cases, the researchers are typically allotted specific days and times to conduct their study. If the researchers are not prepared to collect data on the day and time arranged with the external institutions, their opportunity to do so may be forever lost. Many institutions will not be willing to further assist a researcher who has failed to show up in the past. Thus, it is often important for researchers to have a backup plan in the event that an emergency or other unforeseen circumstance prevents them from arriving at the institution with the materials necessary to conduct their study.

You too should consider yourself to be a researcher with a rare, one-time opportunity to collect data for your team's study. As such, you should be equipped with a backup plan in case one of your team members does not show up for this meeting with his/her share of the required materials. If a team member has proven unreliable at previous meetings, do not count on him/her to bring imperative materials. If for any reason (even a valid medical excuse for one of your members) your team is not prepared to collect data for your study, your team members will likely be given no opportunity to collect data, you will be asked to spend the lab meeting time participating in other groups' studies, and the instructor may give a deduction to ALL members of your team. You are expected to work as a team and to have backup plans in place for unforeseen circumstances.

Use the space below to list which team members will be responsible for bringing the various materials. Ideally, two members should be responsible for bringing each set of materials in case one has an emergency preventing him/her from attending the lab. If you haven't already done so, use the first page of this guide to record each other's cell phone numbers so that you can reach one another in the event of an emergency.

Materials	Team Member(s) Responsible

Lab 3 worksheet

Answer each of the following questions immediately after your team finishes collecting data for your study. Use the space below to fill in your answers. The information you record here will be useful when you are preparing the discussion section of your research report.

1. Provide a brief description of any unexpected problems/issues you encountered when running your study and describe how you dealt with each.

2. Describe any confounds you identified when running your experiment and how you could change your procedure/design to eliminate them. (Note: it is common for confounds to be detected in the early stages of a study and for researchers to adjust the procedure to eliminate them. Remember, no person and no research design is perfect.) Alternatively, if you used a correlational design, identify any third variables that may have had an influence on the relationship under investigation.

3. If you could run your study again, what changes would you make and why would you make those changes?

Before leaving the third lab meeting, your research team should briefly discuss your plan for sharing the data. You may choose to photocopy your response sheets and have team members enter their own data, or to nominate one member to enter the data in Microsoft Excel and email it to the remaining group members. If you choose to nominate a member to enter the data, you should have another member double-check the data to ensure that they are entered properly and that any data entry errors are caught and corrected.

Use the following worksheet to identify which team members will be responsible for entering, checking, and distributing the data. Identify a group due date, which should represent the date the task should be completed and submitted to the team. Also identify the class due date, which should represent the date the instructor has designated for the fourth lab meeting. Be sure to leave enough time between the group due date and the class due date for your team members to have a chance to review the data.

This worksheet is intended to help you to form a contract with your group. Members should sign their names next to tasks for which they volunteer to acknowledge their responsibility for completing the tasks on or before the group due date identified. Instead of dividing up the duties, you may wish to meet as a team to enter the data in a spreadsheet, check the entered data, and distribute them to all of the team members.

Names and Signatures of Members Responsible for Entering the Data:

Group Due Date: **Class Due Date:**

Names and Signatures of Members Responsible for Checking and Distributing the Data:

Group Due Date: **Class Due Date:**

Note: When entering your data in Microsoft Excel, you should be sure to enter the data from each group/condition in a separate column. Label each column with the name of the group/condition so you can easily distinguish the data corresponding to each. The values you enter below each column heading should represent the score each individual in that group/condition received on the dependent variable. Thus, if you had two groups or conditions with 10 people in each group, you should have two columns with 10 rows of data. Illustrations of how to enter data are provided in Appendix 2.

DATA SUMMARY

Objectives

- To learn how to summarize your data using descriptive statistics
- To learn how to graph your results

In this lab, you will learn the fundamentals of descriptive statistics. You will learn which descriptive statistics are appropriate for summarizing your data, how to calculate these descriptive statistics, and how to meaningfully depict your findings using graphs.

Advanced Preparation

Before coming to this lab meeting, you should complete the following three tasks:

- ☐ Ensure your research team's data are entered into Microsoft Excel and double-checked.
- ☐ Review the sections in your textbook and lecture notes on descriptive statistics and graphs as well as the information in this chapter of the guide.
- ☐ Determine which scale of measure (i.e., nominal) was used to measure your dependent variable.

After completing each of the tasks listed above, check the corresponding box to indicate its completion. You will be prepared for the fourth lab once all three boxes are checked.

Statistics

©Termit, 2010. Used under license from Shutterstock, Inc.

Statistics tend to frighten a lot of people. This is likely because many people don't get the opportunity to learn how to use statistics and people tend to fear the unknown. Moreover, the symbols used to represent many statistics can be foreign-looking and intimidating. You will soon discover that descriptive statistics are fairly easy and certainly nothing to fear. The skills you will learn in this lab will make your transition into any introductory statistics course a lot smoother and should help you develop confidence in your ability to calculate, report, and understand descriptive statistics.

Statistics are used for two purposes. Descriptive statistics are used to summarize data. The mean, median, mode, percentage, standard deviation, and correlation are all generally considered descriptive statistics because we use them to summarize, characterize or otherwise describe our data. Inferential statistics (e.g., chi-square, *t*-test) are used to make inferences about a population on the basis of sample data. In other words, they are used to indicate whether an effect we find in a study (from a sample) is likely to represent a real effect (one that would be found if we tested the entire population) or whether it is likely to simply be the result of chance or random error. A statistically significant effect is one that has a low probability (usually a 5% chance or less) of being a result of chance alone.

Statistical significance can only be determined using inferential statistics. Since introducing the principles of inferential statistics is typically beyond the scope of most introductory research methods courses, we will focus only on descriptive statistics, on providing useful characterizations or summaries of your data. It is important to note that without the use of inferential statistics to determine whether your effect has a low probability of being due to random error or chance, it will be inappropriate for you to conclude that your effect is *statistically significant*. Rather than focusing on determining whether the effect you detect in your study is statistically significant, you should instead simply consider the size of the effect. That is, you should simply consider the size of the difference between percentages or means or the magnitude of the correlation coefficient. Large effects (i.e., large differences between the groups and large correlation coefficients) are more likely to be significant: that is, large effects are less likely to be due to random error alone.

Determining Which Descriptive Statistics Are Appropriate to Calculate and Report

The type of descriptive statistics you will need to calculate and report will depend on (a) the type of design you used and (b) the measurement scale you used for your dependent variable. A brief description of the types of descriptive statistics that are most appropriate to calculate for different research designs and different scales of measure is provided below.

Experimental Design or Non-Experimental Design with Distinct Groups or Conditions

If you used an experimental design (e.g., posttest only design, pretest-posttest design) or a non-experimental design in which you had distinct groups or conditions (e.g., non-equivalent control groups design), then you will need to calculate the same descriptive statistic(s) separately for each group or condition and then compare the values of the statistic(s) across the groups or conditions. This comparison across groups/conditions is usually made using inferential statistics because they allow us to determine whether the difference is statistically significant. Once again, since you will not be using inferential statistics, you will not be able to determine whether a difference across your groups or conditions is *statistically significant,* but you should use your judgment to determine whether the difference across your groups/conditions is large enough to likely represent a real effect, one that is produced by your independent variable.

Review of Scales of Measure

Nominal Scales: *Data measured on a nominal scale are categorical or qualitative in nature. While numbers may be used to represent or code the different groups or categories, they do not represent a numerical quantity. Examples of variables measured on a nominal scale are gender, ethnicity, brand of jeans, and undergraduate major.*

Ordinal Scales: *Data measured on an ordinal scale represent rank orders where the difference between ranks is not necessarily the same. In other words, the difference between rankings of 1st and 2nd is not necessarily the same as the difference between rankings of 3rd and 4th. Examples include rank ordering a set of pictures according to attractiveness and rank ordering a list of TV shows from least to most entertaining.*

Interval Scales: *Data measured on an interval scale are quantitative in nature. The numbers used represent real numbers that designate actual amounts. As such, the magnitude of difference between any two values is the same: that is, the difference between 1 and 2 is the same as the difference between*

(continued)

5 and 6. However, data measured on an interval scale do not have an absolute zero point to represent the absence of the variable. Examples include temperature (in Celsius or Fahrenheit) and most psychological states and traits.*

Ratio Scales: *Data measured on ratio scales are similar to those measured on interval scales in that they are quantitative in nature and the numbers used represent real numbers that designate real amounts and reflect relative differences in magnitude. However, unlike interval scales, ratio scales do have an absolute zero point that represents the absence of the variable. Examples of variables measured on a ratio scale include height, weight, age, and time. Concretely, the difference between 2 seconds and 3 seconds is the same as the difference between 4 seconds and 5 seconds. Also 0 seconds indicates no time.*

*Note: There is some debate about whether the Likert-type rating scales researchers typically use to measure psychological states and traits are best categorized as ordinal or interval, because we can't be sure whether participants perceive the difference between intervals on the rating scale to be equal (e.g., that the perceived difference between agree and strongly agree is the same as the perceived difference between disagree and strongly disagree). However, most researchers categorize the measurement of psychological traits and states as interval scales, because the intention is for participants to treat the intervals as equal and because more informative statistics can be applied to data that were measured using interval scales.

Important Note on the Pretest-Posttest Design: If you used a pretest-posttest design, you will need to calculate and report the same descriptive statistic(s) separately for each group/condition for both the pretest and the posttest. If the pretest scores are similar across the groups/conditions, then you will be able to simply directly compare the values of the descriptive statistic(s) on the posttest. If the pretest scores are not similar across the groups/conditions, then you will need to calculate change scores for each participant (by subtracting each participant's pretest score from his/her posttest score), calculate the descriptive statistic(s) on the change scores, and then compare the values of the descriptive statistic(s) across the groups/conditions.

Different descriptive statistics will need to be calculated depending on whether your dependent variable was measured on a nominal or ordinal scale or on an interval or ratio scale. If you are unsure which scale your dependent variable was measured on, you should first attempt to identify it by consulting the information provided in the box above. Once you have identified the scale of measure used for your dependent variable, review the information provided below to determine the descriptive statistic(s) that are most appropriate for you to calculate and report.

Nominal and Ordinal Scale Data

If your dependent variable was measured using either a nominal scale or an ordinal scale, then you will need to calculate and compare percentages and/or modes across your groups or conditions. Modes tend to be less informative than percentages, so if they are calculated and reported, they should be reported in conjunction with, rather than instead of, percentages. It should be noted that in some circumstances when the dependent variable was measured using an ordinal scale, it is also appropriate to calculate the median. However, since the median rarely provides a meaningful description of the results of experiments with ordinal dependent variables, it will not be reviewed in much detail here.

As you may discover, ordinal scale data are the most difficult to summarize in a meaningful way, and the most appropriate descriptive statistic to calculate and report (i.e., percentages, modes, and/or medians) will vary depending on your research question and the goals of your experiment. If your dependent variable was measured by having participants rank order items, then you will need to review what each descriptive statistic represents and use your judgment to determine which is (or are) the most appropriate to calculate and report given your research goals. Your instructor or teaching assistant should be able to help guide your decision.

Interval and Ratio Scale Data

If your dependent variable was measured using either an interval or a ratio scale, then in most cases you will need to calculate means and standard deviations for each group/condition and compare the values of the means across the groups or conditions. The mean provides an indicator of central tendency: it indicates on average how people in the various groups/conditions responded or scored on the dependent variable. While the mean is an informative indicator of central tendency, it is usually also desirable to know how much variability there is in the responses or scores. As such, standard deviations are typically reported along with the means to indicate how dispersed or spread apart the various scores in each group are from each other. Note however, that while means are customarily compared across groups/conditions, it is not typically meaningful to provide a comparison of the standard deviations across the groups or conditions.

The mean and standard deviation are not as appropriate to calculate and report when the data contain extreme scores. Extreme scores are scores that are much higher or lower than all of the other scores in the distribution. They are outliers that don't fit with the rest of the distribution of scores. Extreme scores distort the value of the mean and standard deviation because the value of every score is used in their calculation. If the data set contains one extremely high score, then the mean will be higher than it should be to accurately reflect the data as a whole. If the data set contains one extremely low score, then the mean will be lower than it should be to accurately reflect the data as a whole. Extreme scores also distort the value of the standard deviation by inflating its value. In contrast, extreme scores have very little influence on the median. As such, the median becomes the most appropriate descriptive statistic to compute and compare across groups/conditions when the data contain one or more extreme scores. An alternative way to deal with extreme scores is to exclude them from the analysis: that is, to delete all of the data from the participant who produced the extreme score(s) and then continue to calculate the means and standard deviations on the data from the reduced sample.

Statistics Is an Art and a Science

You may discover that the same data can sometimes be analyzed in different ways. For instance, if you wanted to examine the relationship between gender and memory test performance, you could assign each gender a code (e.g., males a 1 and females a 2) and then correlate gender with memory test scores. Alternatively, you could view the genders as distinct groups and proceed by computing and comparing the mean memory test scores of males and females. In a case like this, the latter option is preferable. If possible, avoid using correlation to analyze your results because it is less intuitive and less amenable to clear graphical representation. If you can break your participants into distinct groups, you should do so and provide a comparison of the same descriptive statistic (e.g., mean, mode, percentage) across your groups.

Correlational Design

If you used a correlational design, where you simply measured two variables as they naturally occur, without manipulating anything and without dividing participants into distinct groups/conditions, then you will need to compute a correlation coefficient. Typically, correlation coefficients are computed on two variables that have been measured on interval or ratio scales. However, correlation coefficients can also be computed on variables measured on nominal scales with only two categories, variables measured on ordinal scales, and combinations of these (e.g., one variable measured on an ordinal scale and the other measured on an interval scale). Note that correlation does not offer a meaningful analysis for variables measured on a nominal scale with more than two categories (e.g., ethnicity).

Summary of Appropriate Descriptive Statistics to Calculate and Report

Research Design Containing Distinct Groups or Conditions
Nominal Scale—Percentages and/or Modes
Ordinal Scale—Percentages, Modes, and/or Medians
Interval or Ratio Scale—Means and Standard Deviations or Medians

Correlational Design (No Distinct Groups or Conditions)
Nominal (with 2 levels), Ordinal, Interval, or Ratio Scale—Correlation Coefficient

Computing Descriptive Statistics

Percentages

To compute percentages for nominal scale data, you simply need to tally up the number of participants in each group who selected or represented the category of interest (or each category), divide that value by the total number of participants in the group, and then multiply the outcome by 100. To compute percentages for ordinal scale data, you need to tally up the number of participants in each group who ranked the item (or items) of interest 1st, divide each sum by the total number of participants in the corresponding group, and then multiply each outcome by 100. Depending on the research question, it may also be reasonable to compute and report the percentage of participants who ranked an item (or items) of interest 2nd, 3rd, etc. See Example 1 in Appendix 2 for a demonstration of the calculation of percentages.

© Pedro Tavres, 2010. Used under license from Shutterstock, Inc.

Modes

The mode is the most frequently occurring score. In the case of a nominal dependent variable, it is the most frequently occurring category selected or represented by members in each group. In the case of an ordinal dependent variable, the mode is the item most frequently ranked 1st (and sometimes 2nd, 3rd, etc.) by members in each group/condition. If a tie is detected in any one of the groups/conditions, then both categories/items are reported as the modes and the distribution is said to be bimodal. See Example 1 in Appendix 2 for an illustration of the calculation of modes.

Medians

The median is the centermost score: the score that divides the distribution in half. To calculate the median by hand, you first need to rank order the scores (from largest to smallest or smallest to largest). If there is an odd number of scores in the group/condition, then the score in the very middle is the median. If there is an even number of scores in the group/condition, then the median is the mean (i.e., the average) of the two middlemost scores. While it is very easy to calculate the median by hand, you should be aware that it can also be calculated using Microsoft Excel. To learn how to compute the median in Excel, refer to the information on using formulas in Microsoft Excel provided on page 43. Also see Example 3 in Appendix 2 for a demonstration of the calculation of medians in Excel.

Means

Mean is just another word for average. Thus, to compute the means, you simply need to compute the average score in each group/condition. Specifically, to compute the means, sum together the relevant scores in the group/condition and then divide the sum by the total number of scores that were summed (the total number of participants in the group/condition). While the mean is easy enough to calculate by hand, it can also be calculated using Microsoft Excel. To learn how to compute the mean in Excel, refer to the information on using formulas in Microsoft Excel provided on page 43. Also see Example 2 in Appendix 2 for a demonstration of the calculation of means in Excel.

Standard Deviations

The standard deviation provides an index of the average distance of scores from the mean. A low standard deviation indicates that the scores in a group are all quite similar, falling close to the mean. A high standard deviation indicates that the scores in a group vary a lot from each other, with some falling close to the mean and others falling far from the mean. An illustration is provided in the box below. Learning how to calculate the standard deviation by hand is beyond the scope of the labs. Fortunately, standard deviations can easily be calculated in Excel. To learn how to compute the standard deviation in Excel, refer to the information on using formulas in Microsoft Excel provided on page 43. Also see Example 2 in Appendix 2 for a demonstration of the calculation of standard deviations in Excel.

Consider the following two sets of scores:

Set 1: 5, 6, 4, 5, 5, 6, 4, 5, 6, 4
Set 2: 5, 9, 1, 3, 5, 8, 0, 9, 2, 8

Both sets of scores have a mean of 5. However Set 1 has a standard deviation of .82, meaning that on average scores are .82 units away from the mean. In contrast, Set 2 has a standard deviation of 3.40, meaning that on average scores are 3.40 units away from the mean. You should notice that compared to the scores in Set 2, those in Set 1 have less variability. That is, the scores in Set 1 are all quite close to each other and to the mean.

Correlation Coefficients

Correlation coefficients are appropriate to calculate when two variables were simply measured without dividing participants into distinct groups/conditions or manipulating anything. Correlation coefficients express the direction and strength of the relationship between two variables. Positive coefficients indicate that a positive relationship exists between the variables: that as one variable increases, so does the other. Negative coefficients indicate that an inverse relationship exists between the variables: that as one variable increases, the other decreases. Correlation coefficients can range from –1 to +1. A coefficient of –1 or +1 indicates a perfect relationship between the variables, while a coefficient of 0 indicates that there is no relationship between the variables. Most coefficients fall between –1 and 0 or 0 and +1. The further the coefficient is from 0, the stronger the magnitude of relationship between the variables. Correlation coefficients between 0 and .30 (or 0 and –.30) are generally interpreted as small, those between .30 and .50 (or –.30 and –.50) are generally interpreted as moderate, and those above .50 (or below –.50) are generally interpreted as large. Since it is very tedious to calculate correlation coefficients by hand, researchers almost always rely on computer software for their computations. To learn how to compute a correlation coefficient in Excel, refer to the information on using formulas in Microsoft Excel provided on page 43. Also see Example 4 in Appendix 2 for a demonstration of the calculation of a correlation coefficient in Excel.

Using Formulas in Microsoft Excel

Excel makes calculations of descriptive statistics extremely easy. The following formulas will allow you to calculate the reviewed descriptive statistics quickly and without error.

The formula to calculate a **median** *is:* **=MEDIAN()**

The formula to calculate a **mean** *is:* **=AVERAGE()**

The formula to calculate a **standard deviation** *is:* **=STDEV()**

Before using the above formulas, you will need to ensure your data are organized in Excel such that the data (i.e., participants' scores on the dependent variable) from each group or condition are organized together in their own separate column. Once the data are organized, type the formula into a blank cell and place your cursor in the middle of the empty parentheses in the formula by clicking between them. Next, drag your cursor over the data points you want included in the calculation (start by clicking on the first score and then drag down to the last score). Once the parentheses contain a display of the range of cells containing the relevant data, press Enter. The value of the descriptive statistic will then be displayed in place of the formula you typed.

The = sign in the formulas indicates to Excel that you are inputting a formula, the word or abbreviation (e.g., MEDIAN, STDEV) informs Excel what staistic you want to calculate, and the information in the parentheses informs Excel which scores you want included in the calculation.

The formula to calculate a **correlation coefficient** *is:* **=CORREL()**

Before using the formula, you will need to ensure that your data are organized in two separate columns in Excel, with one column for each variable that was measured. Since correlation considers the degree to which participants' scores on one variable are related to their scores on another variable, **it is very important that each row contains the same participant's data on both variables.** *Once the data are organized, type the formula into a blank cell and place your cursor in the middle of the empty parentheses by clicking between them. Next, drag your cursor over the data points contained in the first column (the scores on the first variable), starting with the first score and ending with the last score. Once the parentheses contain a display of the range of cells containing the data for the first variable, enter a comma (,) and then drag your cursor over the data points contained in the second column (the scores on the second variable). Once the parentheses contain a complete display of the ranges of cells containing the data on which you want to calculate the correlation coefficient, press Enter. After you press Enter, the value of the correlation coefficient should be displayed in the cell in place of the formula you typed.*

Graphing Your Results

Graphs provide an ideal means to depict the results of a study because they are easy to extract information from quickly. While in some cases it is appropriate to display results in a table[1], graphs tend to be preferred by readers over tables because they are less tedious to look at and extract information from. For that reason, you are encouraged to graph your data and to present at least one graphical representation of the results of your study in your research report.

---

[1] Tables should be used when there are many statistics to report.

Depending on your research design and the nature of your data, different types of graphs will be appropriate to construct. Note that in almost all cases, graphs of frequency distributions will not be a meaningful way for you to depict the results of your study. This is because frequency distributions do not permit your reader to compare the performance of the groups/conditions quickly in a glance. Use the information provided below to identify the most appropriate and meaningful type of graph to construct to represent your data.

Review of Graphs

X and Y Axes: *Graphs contain two axes: the X axis (the abscissa) and the Y axis (the ordinate). The X axis is the horizontal axis, and it is customarily used to present the different levels of the* **independent variable**. *The Y axis is the vertical axis, and it is customarily used to present the* **dependent variable**. *More precisely the Y axis is used to display the values of the descriptive statistic used to summarize the data (e.g., percentage, mode, median, or mean).*

Both axes must be labeled in a meaningful way. If your reader has to spend time trying to determine what each axis represents, then the graph no longer serves its purpose of conveying your results in a simple glance.

Legends: *When it is not clear from the labels on the X axis what the various bars or lines represent, legends are necessary. If more than one set of bars or more than one line is presented on your graph, a legend providing information on what each set of bars or line represents should be included.*

Graphing Several Results: *If you want to graph more than one set of descriptive statistics (e.g., means and medians), you will need to create separate graphs for each (one graph with the values of the means for each group/condition and a separate graph with the values of the medians for each group/condition). Standard deviations are not customarily graphed, although they may be included on graphs in the form of error bars.*

Each graph you create should have the data from all of the various groups or conditions. Do not create separate graphs for each of your groups or conditions because your reader will not be able to compare the performance of the groups/conditions in a glance.

Bar Graphs

Bar graphs are used to present the results of experiments in which the levels of the independent variable are categorical. The individual bars on the graph are meant to represent each of the different groups/conditions. The height of each bar indicates the value of the descriptive statistic of interest (e.g., percentage, mean) for that group/condition. The discrete bars used in bar graphs are meant to represent the categorical nature of the variable plotted on the X axis (the independent variable). Since most experiments contain distinct groups/conditions, bar graphs tend to be the most commonly used type of graph.

For example, assume you were interested in whether presenting objects in colour, rather than in black and white, influences people's ability to remember them. Further assume that you manipulated the colour in which pictures of objects were presented to participants such that participants in one group were shown 10 pictures of objects in colour while participants in a separate group were shown 10 pictures of the same objects in black and white. In this case, a bar graph would be most appropriate to depict your results. This is because the levels of the independent variable represent different types of pictures, making it a categorical rather than continuous variable. An appropriate bar graph to depict the results of an experiment like the one described is shown below.

You should note that there is a separate bar to represent each of the distinct groups: one to represent the group that was shown pictures of objects in colour and one to represent the group that was shown pictures of objects in black and white. As indicated by the label on the Y axis, the height of each bar represents the mean number of objects that participants in the group recalled. You can see that participants in the "Colour" group recalled a mean of 9.2 objects, while participants in the "Black and White" group recalled a mean of 7.5 objects.

Line Graphs

Line graphs are used to present the results of experiments in which the levels of the independent variable are continuous rather than discrete or categorical in nature. The markers (i.e., points) on the line represent the various groups/conditions. The height of each marker indicates the value of the descriptive statistic of interest for that group/condition. The continuous line connecting the markers is meant to reflect the continuous nature of the variable plotted on the X axis (the independent variable).

For example, assume you were interested in whether the amount of time spent studying objects influences memory test performance. Assume you manipulated the amount of time participants had to study a series of 10 objects such that participants in one group had 1 second to study each object while participants in another group had 2 seconds to study each object. In this case, a line graph would be appropriate to depict your results. This is because the levels of the independent variable represent differences in time, making it a continuous rather than discrete variable. An appropriate line graph to depict the results of an experiment like the one described is shown below.

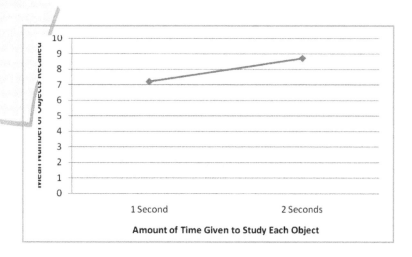

Note that the line has separate markers to represent each of the groups: one for the group that was given 1 second to study objects and another for the group that was given 2 seconds. The label on the Y axis indicates that the height of each marker represents the mean number of objects that participants in the group recalled. It is clear that those who were given 1 second to study each object recalled a mean of 7.2 objects, while those who were given 2 seconds to study each object recalled a mean of 8.7 objects.

Scatter Plots

Scatter plots are typically used to graphically depict the results of correlational studies. Each individual point on the scatter plot represents the scores of one participant on both variables that were measured. The height of the point represents the participant's score on the Y variable, while the horizontal location of the point represents the participant's score on the X variable. Since correlational designs do not contain an independent or dependent variable, it is arbitrary which variable is plotted on the X axis and which is on the Y axis. Note however, that if the results are intended to be used to make predictions of the value of one variable based on the value of another variable, then the variable that will be predicted (the outcome variable) is customarily placed on the Y axis and the variable on which the prediction will be based (the predictor variable) is placed on the X axis.

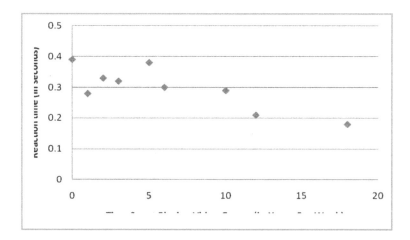

For instance, assume you were interested in the relationship between the number of hours per week people spend playing video games and their reaction time. Further assume that you simply asked people how many hours a week they spend playing video games and that you used an online reaction time test to measure their reaction time. In this case, where nothing is manipulated and no groups are formed, a scatter plot would be most appropriate to depict your results.

You should note that there is one point on the graph for each participant and each point represents a participant's scores on the two variables that were measured. The clearly labeled Y axis allows us to easily see that the height of each point represents the participant's reaction time in seconds. The clearly labeled X axis allows us to easily see that the horizontal placement of each point represents the time spent playing video games in hours per week. By looking at the top leftmost point, you can see that one participant reported spending 0 hours per week playing video games and had a reaction time of .38 seconds.

Research Methods in Psychology

Constructing Graphs Using Microsoft Excel

Bar and Line Graphs

Graphs are fairly easy to construct using Microsoft Excel. The key to creating any graph in Excel is good organization of the data. To create a bar or line graph, you will need to do the following[2]:

1. The values of the descriptive statistic you want to graph (e.g., percentages, modes, medians, or means) first need to be organized together in a single row with the names of the corresponding groups/conditions appearing immediately above each value. Note: If you used a pretest-posttest design and you want to graph the pretest and the posttest results, then you will need to organize the data into two rows. One row should contain the values of the descriptive statistic on the pretest and a separate row (appearing immediately below the first row) should contain the values of the descriptive statistic on the posttest. Label the rows "Pretest" and "Posttest."

2. Highlight the names of the groups/conditions and the values of the descriptive statistics you want graphed and click on the Insert tab in the top toolbar. A new toolbar will now appear with options to create various types of graphs.

3. To create a bar graph, you should click on the Column icon (since it is customary to present the bars in a vertical rather than horizontal manner). To create a line graph, you should click on the Line icon. A series of options for different types of graphs will now appear.

4. It is best to keep your graph simple and traditional, so for a bar graph you are advised to select the first option in the series (the simplest 2D graph). For a line graph, you are advised to select the option in the second row of the first column (a 2D graph with markers). A graph will now appear, but it won't have a labeled Y axis.

5. To create a clear and well labeled graph, you will need to use the Chart Layouts option, which should now appear in your toolbar. For a bar graph, you are advised to select the option presented in the last column of the third row (Layout 9). For a line graph, you are advised to select the option presented in the last row of the first column (Layout 10).

6. Now your graph will have places to label each of the axes (Axis Title), to create a legend (Series1), and to name the graph (Chart Title).

    i. To label the axes, double-click on the Axis Title, type the name of the axis, and press Enter.

    ii. It is not customary to name graphs presented in research reports; as such, you may delete the Chart Title by clicking on it and pressing Delete.

    iii. If the information presented in the Series legend is redundant with that provided on the X axis, you should delete it by clicking on it and pressing Delete. If it is not clear what the bars or lines represent in your graph (if you have more than one set of bars or more than one line), you

---

[2] The following steps are based on Microsoft Excel 2007. Different versions of Excel will have slightly different options and procedures for creating graphs.

can change the title of the Series legend by clicking on it, typing in a new title, and pressing Enter.

Note: Many other features of the graph can be manipulated. For instance, the colours can be changed using the options in the toolbar. The gridlines can be removed by right-clicking on a gridline and pressing Delete. The X axis can also be changed by right-clicking on it, clicking Format Axis, and changing the minimum and maximum values. You should spend some time clicking on the various components of the graphs to reveal the various options available to personalize your graph.

See Examples 1–3 in Appendix 2 for demonstrations of the steps to creating a bar graph.

Scatter Plots

To create a scatter plot in Excel, you will need to do the following[3]:

1. Organize the data such that the raw data (individuals' scores) appear in two separate columns (one column for each variable that was measured). Since each point plotted on the scatter plot should represent one participant's scores on both variables, it is very important that each row contains the same participant's data on both variables.
2. Highlight all of the data points (both columns) you want graphed and click on the Insert tab in the top toolbar. A new toolbar will now appear with options to create various types of graphs.
3. To create a scatter plot, you should click on the Scatter icon.
4. A series of options for different types of graphs will now appear. You need to select the first option (the one that doesn't contain any lines). A graph will now appear, but it won't have labeled axes.
5. To create a clear and well labeled graph, you will need to use the Chart Layouts option, which should now appear in your toolbar. You will need to select the first option (Layout 1).
6. Now your graph will have a place to label each of the axes (Axis Title), to create a legend (Series1), and name the graph (Chart Title).
    i. To label the axes, double-click on the Axis Title, type the name of the axis, and press Enter.
    ii. It is not customary to name graphs presented in research reports or to include a legend on a scatter plot; as such, you may delete the Chart Title and Series legend by clicking on each and hitting Delete.

See Example 4 in Appendix 2 for a demonstration of the steps to creating a scatter plot.

---

[3] The following steps are based on Microsoft Excel 2007. Different versions of Excel will have slightly different options and procedures for creating graphs.

Lab 4 worksheet

After reviewing the information in this chapter, you should answer each of the following questions. The information you record here will be useful when you are preparing the results section of your research report.

1. What was your dependent variable and how was it measured?

    a. Identify which type of scale was used to measure your dependent variable.
        ☐ Nominal
        ☐ Ordinal
        ☐ Interval
        ☐ Ratio

2. Which descriptive statistic(s) will you calculate and report in the results section of your research report?
    ☐ Percentages
    ☐ Modes
    ☐ Means
    ☐ Medians
    ☐ Standard Deviations
    ☐ Correlation Coefficient

3. How will you perform these calculations? If you plan to use Microsoft Excel, what formula(s) will you need to use? [e.g., =AVERAGE()]?

4. How did you manipulate the independent variable (what were the levels of your independent variable)?

    a. What type of graph will you use to depict your findings?
        ☐ Bar Graph
        ☐ Line Graph
        ☐ Scatter Plot

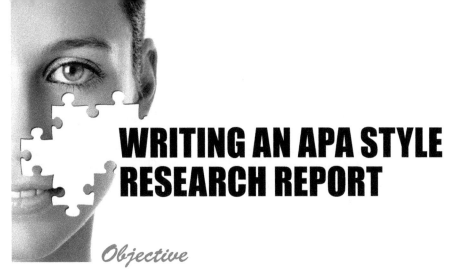

WRITING AN APA STYLE RESEARCH REPORT

Objective

To learn how to write an APA style research report

In this lab, you will learn how to write a research report using the style of the American Psychological Association (APA). You will learn what information should be contained in the various sections of your report, how to format your report, and how to properly cite and reference previous work.

© JupiterImages Corporation

Advanced Preparation

Before coming to this lab meeting, you should complete the following two tasks:

- ❏ Review the section in your textbook pertaining to writing a research report (check your text's appendix for this information if it does not appear in a chapter) as well as the information in this chapter of the guide.
- ❏ Create a rough outline or draft of your paper and identify any questions/problems you have.

After completing each of the tasks listed above, check the corresponding box to indicate its completion. You will be prepared for the fifth lab once both boxes are checked.

APA Style

APA style refers to a specific writing style. Although developed by the American Psychological Association (APA), this writing style is required by scientific journals in many fields. Journals publishing in the fields of psychology, business, economics, education, sociology, nursing, and many others require submitted papers to be prepared in APA style.

This chapter is intended to provide an overview of the information that should be contained in the various sections of an APA style research report, a brief description of some of the APA formatting rules, and information on properly citing and referencing previous work. This chapter is not intended to provide exhaustive information on the various details of APA style and should be used in conjunction with the most recent edition of the *Publication Manual of the American Psychological Association*[4].

Sections of an APA Style Report

There are eight main sections in an APA style research report. A description of each of these sections and the information that should be contained within each is provided below.

1. Title Page

The title page is intended to provide the reader with information on the title of the research report as well as information about the authors of the report. It should contain the following:

---

[4] The sixth edition of the *Publication Manual of the American Psychological Association* (2009) was the most recent edition at the time this guide was published.

Title

A brief but informative title should be provided. A good title conveys the main idea of the paper with style.

Authors' Names

A complete list of the contributing authors should be provided. Typically the order of authors is determined by their amount of contribution. For our purposes, you should list yourself as first author and your team members as subsequent authors. You should organize your team members either in order of their contributions to the project or alphabetically.

Institutional Affiliation

The institutional affiliation is the name of the institution at which the research was conducted and/or with which the authors are affiliated. You should provide the name of your university.

Running Head

The running head should contain an abbreviated form of your title. It should not exceed 50 characters (including spaces). It will appear in the header of every page of your report.

Author Note

Your name and contact information (your university department mailing address and your email address) should be provided on the title page. Typically, APA style also requires complete information on the author's departmental affiliation and acknowledgments of research grants and sources of funding, but since your departmental affiliation will appear in your university mailing address and your project was not funded, you do not need to include that information.

2. Abstract

The purpose of the abstract is to give potential readers enough information about the report to determine whether it contains information of interest or relevance to them. Your abstract should briefly summarize the body (the introduction, method, results, and discussion sections) of your report. You should note that it is often easiest to write the abstract after writing the body of the report. The abstract should be between 100 and 150 words.

3. Introduction

The introduction should set the stage for your research report. To capture the immediate interest and attention of your readers, it is often useful to begin with a brief discussion of a real-world context related to your research question. The beginning section of your introduction should also contain a mini literature review in which you provide a brief overview of at least two previous related studies. The purpose of reviewing previous research is to place your study in the larger context of the literature

on the topic. As such, you should ensure that the previous research you discuss is directly relevant and related to your study. While original research questions tend to be of greater interest to readers (and journal editors), you were not expected to come up with a research question that has not previously been addressed. If previous research has examined a research question similar (or identical) to yours, you should be sure to identify and review it in your introduction.

After reviewing previous relevant research, you should provide an explanation of the purpose of your study (i.e., identify your specific research question). If you can identify how your study improves or extends upon the previous research you discussed, you should do so. Alternatively, you should provide some explanation of why your study is interesting or important. Finally, you should explain your hypothesis, and if applicable, provide some justification for your hypothesis.

4. Method

The method section should give the reader a clear sense of how your study was conducted. Ideally, it should provide the reader with enough information to conduct an exact replication of your study. It is customary to include the following subsections in the method section:

Participants

The subsection on participants should contain a description of who the participants were (e.g., undergraduate students), the number of participants in each of the various groups/conditions, and a brief description of how they were sampled (e.g., from an introductory research methods course). If you collected any demographic information from your participants (e.g., age, gender), you should provide a meaningful summary of the information in this section.

Materials

The subsection on materials should contain a description of all of the materials used in your study. If you wish to include pictures or images of any of the materials you used, they should be included in an appendix rather than in the body of the report.

Procedure

The subsection on procedure should identify the type of design used along with a description of the design. It should contain clear descriptions of your independent variable and how it was manipulated as well as your dependent variable and how it was measured. Any controls that you implemented (e.g., random assignment, counterbalancing) should be clearly described.

5. Results

The results section should identify which descriptive statistics were used to summarize the data. If any scoring or coding was necessary, the procedure should be briefly described. The values of the descriptive statistics for each group/condition should be provided in sentence form. Since inferential statistics were not applied, you should be careful not to mention "statistical significance."

Graphs (and/or tables) should only be referred to in this section (e.g., see Figure 1). Actual graphs (and/or tables) should appear only at the end of the report. Similarly, interpretation of the findings should be reserved for the discussion section.

6. Discussion

As implied by its name, the main purpose of the discussion section is to provide a discussion of the study's findings and their implications. It is often useful to begin this section by briefly recapping the purpose of your study and your findings. While the values of descriptive statistics are customarily provided in the results section, an interpretation of these values (and of the magnitude of the differences across groups/conditions) should be provided early in your discussion section.

You should also be sure to include a discussion of how your findings relate to, build on, complement, and/or contradict those of previous research. If your findings contradict those of previous research, you should attempt to identify possible reasons for the contradictory findings (what differed between your studies that could explain the differences in results?). Similarly, if your findings were discordant with your hypothesis, you should attempt to provide an explanation for why your hypothesis was not supported (e.g., was there an unexpected ceiling/floor effect?). You should also attempt to explain why your findings are interesting or important. If possible, relate your findings back to the larger real-world context and describe how they can be applied.

Your discussion section should also contain a section describing the limitations of your study. While it is human nature to try to minimize or conceal our flaws, good scientists recognize that no study is perfect and they openly identify the limitations of their studies. Use this as an opportunity to show off what you know about the limitations of the research design you used (and, if appropriate, describe what attempts you made to minimize them).

Finally, in addition to identifying the limitations associated with your research, you should describe future research that could be conducted that addresses or corrects some of the limitations. For instance, if you used a correlational design, you could discuss your inability to determine a causal relationship between the variables and describe a true experiment that could be conducted and would permit determination of causation. Note that the future research you propose does not just have to correct limitations in your study: it can also be proposed to further extend upon your findings.

7. References

A reference section is included in research reports so that readers can locate and retrieve the primary sources of information given in the report. Any discussion of previous research, facts, definitions, or ideas that are not your own will require a citation in the body of the report as well as a complete reference in the reference section. Without proper referencing, you could be accused of plagiarism.

The reference section of your report should provide complete details of all of the sources that you cited in the body of your report. Each reference should contain the names of the authors, the year of publication, the name of the article (or chapter), the name of the journal (or book), and the page numbers, and, in the case of a book, the name of the publisher and the city in which it was published. The references should appear in alphabetical order according to the first authors' last names. Complete details on how to properly cite and reference various sources are provided below.

8. Figures

Figures are not customarily placed in the body of a report until it is published. Your figures (i.e., graphs) should be placed in a separate section following the reference section of your report. Each figure should be presented on its own page. More details on formatting your figures are provided below.

General APA Format and Style Guidelines

There are some very specific formatting rules and style guidelines for APA style reports. Below is information on some of the most important formatting and style guidelines. You should note that there are several exceptions to these rules, which you should know and adhere to. Complete details on APA style can be found in the most recent edition of the *Publication Manual of the American Psychological Association*.

General Formatting

A 12 point serif font such as Times New Roman should be used. Double-spacing is required throughout the entire report, including the title page. Margins should be set to 1 inch all around. Each new paragraph should be indented. The header of every page should have the content of the running head left justified (in all caps) and the page number right justified. You may need to use section breaks so that the term "Running head:" appears on the title page only.

Title Page

There is a very precise format for the title page. The running head should be left justified in the header of your title page. The content of the running head should be preceded by the words "Running head" and a colon. While only the R in "Running head:" should be capitalized, every letter of the content of the running head should be capitalized.

The title of your report should be centered on the title page. Capitalize the first letter of each important word (or those with more than four letters) in the title. The list of authors should be centered immediately below the title. Next, the name of the institution at which the research was conducted should be centered under the list of authors. Finally, the author note should appear left justified several lines after the institutional affiliation under the centered heading "Author Note." Indent the first line of the sentence containing the correspondence information. A sample title page is shown on page 57.

Running head: SAMPLE APA REPORT 1

Sample APA Style Research Report

Carrie Cuttler

University of British Columbia

Author Note

Correspondence concerning this article should be addressed to Carrie Cuttler, Department of Psychology, University of British Columbia, 2136 West Mall, Vancouver, BC, V6T 1Z4, Canada.

Email: cuttler@fake.email.ubc.ca

Sections and Section Headings

The title page, abstract, reference section, and each figure should begin on a new page. The remaining sections (i.e., introduction, method, results, and discussion) should appear immediately after each other, with no page breaks or extra spaces separating them.

The title of the report should be centered above the introduction but NOT bolded. The headings for the method, results, and discussion sections should be centered and bolded. The headings for the abstract and references should be centered but NOT bolded. Do not italicize, underline, or put any of these headings in all caps. The content of each section should begin one line under its heading.

Subheadings (i.e., participants, materials, procedure) should be left justified and bolded. Do not use italics, do not underline them, and do not put them in all caps. The content of the subsections should begin one line under its heading. An illustrative example is shown on page 58.

Sample APA Style Research Report

The content of the introduction should appear immediately below the centered title. The entire report should be double-spaced and left justified. Margins should be set to 1 inch all around. Each new paragraph should be indented.

Method

Participants

A description of the participants should appear immediately below the left justified bolded subheading.

Materials

A description of the materials should appear immediately below the left justified bolded subheading.

Procedure

A description of the procedure should appear immediately below the left justified bolded subheading.

Results

The content of the results section should appear immediately below the bolded centered heading.

Discussion

The content of the discussion section should appear immediately below the bolded centered heading.

Limitations

Subheadings are not required but can be used sparingly in this section.

References

Specific details on how to create your Reference section are provided in the section on Citations and References.

Figures

Each figure should appear on its own page following the reference section. No headings should appear on the pages depicting the figures. However, each figure should include a brief but informative figure caption that describes what the figure depicts. The figure caption should be preceded by the word "Figure" in italics and the corresponding figure number (also in italics). An illustrative example is shown below.

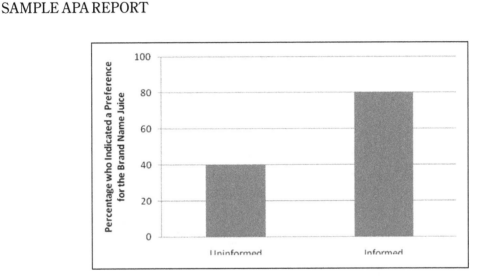

Figure 1. Percentage of participants who indicated a preference for the name brand orange juice as a function of condition (informed vs. uninformed).

Numbers

When numbers from 1–9 are used in the report, they should typically be written out in words (e.g., there were two conditions). When numbers over 10 are used in the report, they should typically appear in numerical format (e.g., there were 10 participants in each condition). An exception is when you are beginning a sentence with a number: in this case, the number that begins the sentence should be written out in words (e.g., Ten students were randomly assigned to the control condition and 10 were assigned to the experimental condition).

Two decimal places should be given when reporting results (e.g., the mean happiness rating in the Self condition was 3.20 while the mean rating in the Other condition was 4.20). If there isn't a decimal remainder, then the whole number can simply be reported (e.g., the name brand orange juice was preferred by 40% of participants in the Uninformed condition and 80% of participants in the Informed condition).

Citations and References

There are very specific methods for citing and referencing other people's work, ideas, and words. Below is information on how to cite authors and how to reference some of the most commonly used sources (i.e., journal articles, books, and chapters in an edited book). Once again, you should note that there are several exceptions to these guidelines, which you should adhere to. Complete details on APA style can be found in the most recent version of the *Publication Manual of the American Psychological Association*.

Citations

Citations appear in the body of the report. A citation should appear immediately after any discussion of other people's work, ideas, definitions, etc., and immediately after quotes. Citations typically contain only the authors' last names and the year of publication. However, citations for quoted material also contain the page number on which the quoted material appeared in the original source.

Citing Work by a Single Author

If you refer to the name of the author in the sentence describing his/her work or idea, then only the year of publication should appear in parentheses next to the author's name. If you don't refer to the name of the author in the sentence describing his/her work or idea, then both the author's last name and the year of publication should appear in parentheses. Examples of each are shown below.

> Cuttler (2010) found that . . .
> . . . was found (Cuttler, 2010).

Citing Work by Two Authors

If you cite work with two authors and you refer to the names of the authors in the sentence describing their work/ideas, then both authors' last names should be separated by the word "and." The year of publication should then appear in parentheses following the authors' names. If you cite work with two authors and you don't refer to the names of the authors in the sentence, then the authors' two last names should appear in parentheses separated by the "&" symbol. The second author's last name should be followed by a comma and the year of publication. Examples of each are shown below.

> Cuttler and Adamson (2010) found that . . .
> . . . was found (Cuttler & Adamson, 2010).

Citing Work by More than Two Authors

If you cite work with between three and five authors, you should include all of the authors' last names the first time you cite the work. For subsequent citations of the same work, you should provide only the last name of the first author followed by "et al." If you cite work with more than five authors, you should include only the last name of the first author followed by "et al." in the first and all subsequent citations. Examples of each are shown below.

First citation of work with three to five authors:

> Cuttler, Adamson, and McLaughlin (2010) found that . . .
> . . . was found (Cuttler, Adamson, & McLaughlin, 2010)

Subsequent citations of same work with three to five authors:

> Cuttler et al. (2010) found that . . .
> . . . was found (Cuttler et al., 2010)

First and subsequent citations of work with more than five authors:

> Cuttler et al. (2010) found that . . .
> . . . was found (Cuttler et al., 2010)

Citing Quoted Material

Citations for quoted material should follow the same general format as described above; however, a comma and the page number of the quoted material should appear immediately after the year of publication. An example is shown below.

> Cuttler, Adamson, and McLaughlin said ". . ." (2010, p. 38)
> ". . ." (Cuttler, Adamson, & McLaughlin, 2010, p. 38)

References

Each citation provided in the body of the report must have a corresponding reference in the reference section, and only cited sources should have a reference in the reference section. The list of references should appear in alphabetical order according to authors' last names. Each reference should be presented using hanging indents. In other words, the first line of each reference should be flush left, but subsequent lines should be indented a half inch.

Journal Articles

References to journal articles should contain the authors' last names and initials (separated by commas), the year of publication (in parentheses), the title of the article, the name of the journal (in italics), the journal volume number (in italics), and the page numbers. The latest edition of the APA manual (the sixth edition) also requires the inclusion of the digital object identifier (DOI) code when one is available. DOIs can often be found on the first page of the journal article when they are available. If a DOI is not available, you simply do not need to include one.

The name of every author should be listed for works with seven authors or less. If the work has more than seven authors, the last names and initials of the first six authors should be followed by an ellipsis (. . .) and then the last name and initial(s) of the last author.

Only the first word of the article title should be capitalized, unless the title contains a colon; then, the first word following the colon should also be capitalized. In contrast, the first letter of every major word in the journal title should be capitalized. Three examples (one for an article written by one author, one for an article written by two

authors, and one for an article written by more than seven authors) are presented below.

>Cuttler, C. (2010). Sample APA style research report. *Journal of Fake Research Reports, 1,* 1–10. doi: 09:2988/fake.doi

>Cuttler, C., & Adamson, C. B. (2010). Sample APA style research report. *Journal of Fake Research Reports, 1,* 1–10. doi: 09:2988/fake.doi

>Cuttler, C., Adamson, C. B., McLaughlin, C. A., Bowen, J. A., Hull, A. J., Guy, J., . . . Adamson, F. S. (2010). Sample APA style research report. *Journal of Fake Research Reports, 1,* 1–10. doi: 09:2988/fake.doi

Books

References to books should contain the authors' last names and initials (separated by commas), the year of publication (in parentheses), the title of the book (in italics), the location of publication and the publisher's name (the last two should be separated by a colon), and a DOI (only if one is available). Only the first letter of the word in the book title should be capitalized, unless the title contains a colon; then, the first word following the colon should also be capitalized. An example is presented below.

>Cuttler, C. (2010). *Research methods in psychology: Student lab guide.* Dubuque, IA: Kendall Hunt Publishing.

Chapters in an Edited Book

References to specific chapters in edited books should contain the chapter authors' last names and initials (separated by commas), the year of publication (in parentheses), the chapter title, the name(s) of the book editor(s) (followed by the abbreviation "Ed." in parentheses), the book title (in italics), the page numbers (in parentheses and preceded by "pp."), and the location of publication and publisher's name (separated by a colon).

Only the first word of the chapter and book titles should be capitalized, unless the titles contain a colon; then, the first word following the colon should also be capitalized. An example is presented below.

>Cuttler, C. (2010). Sample APA style research report. In C. A. Adamson (Ed.), *A fake book on APA style* (pp. 12–24). Dubuque, IA: Kendall Hunt Publishing.

EXAMPLES OF APPROPRIATE RESEARCH QUESTIONS AND DESIGNS

Example 1

Research Question

Does exposing people to information about a brand name affect their preference for the brand name item?

Design

Posttest only design with independent groups.

Method

Each participant will be randomly assigned to one of two conditions: an "Uninformed" control condition or an "Informed" experimental condition. Participants in both conditions will be asked to taste two brands of orange juice (a generic brand and a name brand) and to indicate their preference. Participants in the Uninformed condition will be given no information about the brands of orange juice. Participants in the Informed condition will be told which cup contains the generic brand juice and which contains the brand name juice before being asked to taste each and indicate their preference.

Independent Variable

The information given to participants. Participants in the Uninformed condition will be given no information about the orange juice, while participants in the Informed condition will be told which cup contains the generic brand juice and which contains the name brand juice.

Dependent Variable

The preferred juice (generic brand or name brand).

Controls

Participants will be randomly assigned to participate in one of the two conditions (e.g., the condition assignment will be drawn out of a hat). Both brands of juice will be served in the same unmarked plastic disposable cups. Participants will not see the juice being

poured into the cups from the containers. Juices with similar tastes, colours, and consistencies will be chosen (both will be without pulp and not from concentrate).

Hypothesis

Exposing people to information about a brand name will influence their preference for the brand name item.

Example 2

Research Question

Does recalling a purchase made for someone else make people happier than recalling a purchase they made for themselves?

Design

Pretest-posttest design.

Method

Participants will first be asked to rate how happy they are (pretest) using a 1–5 scale (ranging from not happy to extremely happy). Each participant will then be randomly assigned to one of two conditions: a "Self" condition or an "Other" condition. Participants in the Self condition will be asked to recall and describe in 2–3 sentences the last time they spent $10–$20 on themselves. Participants in the Other condition will be asked to recall and describe in 2–3 sentences the last time they spent $10–$20 on someone else. Immediately after providing the description, participants will be asked to provide another happiness rating (posttest) using the same 1–5 scale.

Independent Variable

The type of purchase recalled. Participants in the Self condition will be asked to recall and describe a purchase they made for themselves. Participants in the Other condition will be asked to recall and describe a purchase they made for someone else.

Dependent Variable

The happiness ratings provided during the posttest. Participants will use a 1–5 scale to rate their happiness (ranging from not happy to extremely happy).

Controls

Participants in each condition will be given the same amount of time to recall and describe the purchase and will use the same scale to rate their happiness. Participants in each condition will be asked to only recall purchases ranging from $10–$20 to control for the amount of money spent. The pretest-posttest design is being used to control for differences in happiness at the onset that random assignment may not take care of because of the expected small sample size.

Hypothesis

Participants who recall making a purchase for someone else will show higher happiness ratings at posttest than participants who recall making a purchase for themselves.

Example 3

Research Question

Does priming participants with a story related to speed increase the speed at which they complete a simple puzzle?

Design

Posttest only design with repeated measures.

Method

Each participant will complete two conditions: a "Speed" condition and a "Neutral" condition. For the Speed condition, participants will be asked to read a short story (three paragraphs) about a speed racer and then to complete a simple puzzle. The story will contain a lot of words related to speed (e.g., *fast, racing, speed, quick, accelerated*). For the Neutral condition, participants will be asked to read a short story (three paragraphs) about a dog and then to complete a simple puzzle. The story will not contain any words related to speed. The number of seconds that it takes each participant to complete the puzzle in each condition will be recorded. However, participants will not know that they are being timed (the experimenter will time them using a concealed stopwatch).

Independent Variable

The story content. A story about speed racing will be used to prime speed in the Speed condition and a story about a dog will be used for the Neutral condition.

Dependent Variable

The number of seconds that it takes participants to complete the puzzle in each condition will be measured using a concealed stopwatch.

Controls

A repeated measures design will be used to ensure that there are no preexisting differences across the conditions with respect to the speed with which participants are able to complete a simple puzzle. The stories participants will read will be of equal length and reading difficulty, and will be printed using the same font and layout, so that the only difference between the conditions is the content of the story that is read. To control for puzzle difficulty, the same puzzle will be used in each condition. To control for order effects, complete counterbalancing will be used. Half of the participants will complete the Speed condition first and the Neutral condition second. The other half of the participants will complete the Neutral condition first and the Speed condition second.

Hypothesis

Participants who are primed with speed will complete the puzzle faster than participants who are not primed with speed.

Example 4

Research Question

Is there a relationship between the number of friends people have on Facebook and the number of friends they socialize with in the real (non-virtual) world?

Design

Correlational design.

Method

Participants will be asked to report (a) how many friends they currently have on Facebook and (b) how many times in the past week they socialized with at least one friend in a non-virtual environment.

Independent Variable

Not applicable. Nothing will be manipulated.

Dependent Variable

Not applicable.

Controls

To increase validity, a computer with Internet access will be available for participants to look up the number of friends they currently have on Facebook.

Hypothesis

There will be a negative correlation between number of friends on Facebook and amount of socialization in the non-virtual world.

EXAMPLES OF COMPUTING DESCRIPTIVE STATISTICS AND GRAPHING RESULTS

The following considers fictional data from the hypothetical experiments described in Appendix 1. You should find and carefully review the example(s) that is/are most similar to your study.

Example 1

This example focused on examining whether exposing people to information about a brand name influences their preference for the brand name item. A posttest only design was used and participants were randomly assigned to one of two conditions. Participants in both conditions were asked to taste both a generic brand and a name brand of orange juice and to indicate their preference. Participants in the "Uninformed" condition were given no information about the brands of juice they were sampling, while those in the "Informed" condition were told which cup contained the brand name juice. Thus, the information given to participants is the independent variable and the preferred brand of juice is the dependent variable. You should recognize that the dependent variable was measured on a nominal scale. As such, we will need to separately calculate and compare percentages and/or modes across the groups.

Organizing the Data in Excel

The data would first need to be organized into two columns in Excel. For this example, one column could be labeled "Uninformed Condition" and the other could be labeled "Informed Condition." Each participant's score on the dependent variable (i.e., the brand each preferred) would then be entered in the appropriate column. Let's assume the data shown in the adjacent figure were obtained from 10 participants. The figure depicts how the data should be entered into Excel.

	A	B
1	**Uninformed Condition**	**Informed Condition**
2	Brand Name	Brand Name
3	Generic Brand	Brand Name
4	Generic Brand	Brand Name
5	Generic Brand	Generic Brand
6	Brand Name	Brand Name

Calculating Descriptive Statistics

Percentages

The data displayed above show that 2 out of 5 participants in the Uninformed condition indicated a preference for the brand name juice, meaning that 40% [(2 ÷ 5) × 100] of people in that condition preferred the brand name juice. The data in the second column show that 4 out of 5 participants in the Informed condition preferred the brand name juice, meaning that 80% [(4 ÷ 5) × 100] of participants in that condition preferred the brand name juice.

Modes

By visually inspecting the data, it is apparent that the generic brand was chosen most frequently by people in the Uninformed condition and that the brand name was chosen most frequently by people in the Informed condition. As such, the mode for the Uninformed condition is generic brand and the mode for the Informed condition is brand name. In this case, where the results provided by the modes and percentages are the same, it would not be necessary to report the modes. As the modes provide less detailed information than the percentages, if modes were reported it would be more appropriate to report them in addition to, rather than in lieu of, the percentages.

Typically an inferential statistics test called chi-square would be used to determine whether the difference in the percentage of participants who preferred the brand name juice in each group is statistically significant. However, since inferential statistics are beyond the scope of the labs, we can simply observe that the percentages of people who preferred the name brand juice are sufficiently different to conclude that exposure to information on brand does have an effect on people's preference for the brand. Specifically, the results suggest that people are more likely to indicate a preference for a brand name product when they are informed that the product is a brand name compared to when they do not have this information.

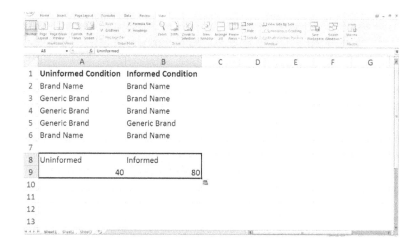

Graphing the Results

Before the results can be graphed, they need to be organized in Excel such that the percentages appear in a single row with the corresponding condition names appearing immediately above. The highlighted area of the adjacent figure demonstrates how the results should be organized in Excel. Since the independent variable is categorical in nature, a bar graph will be most appropriate to depict these results.

To create the bar graph, you would need to highlight the condition names and corresponding percentages, click on the Insert tab in the toolbar, and then click on the Column option in the next toolbar. As shown in the adjacent figure, several options for different types of bar graphs will appear. To create a clean and simple graph, you should select the first type of 2D graph (it is highlighted in the adjacent figure).

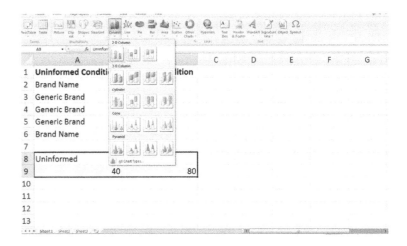

The following graph would then be created. Note that the Y axis is not clearly labeled and an unnecessary legend appears. Also, the Y axis only extends to 90. Since we are considering percentages, the Y axis should extend to 100.

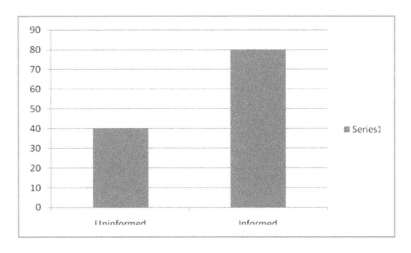

Before you can label the axes, you need to change the layout to Layout 9 using the Chart Layout option depicted in the adjacent figure.

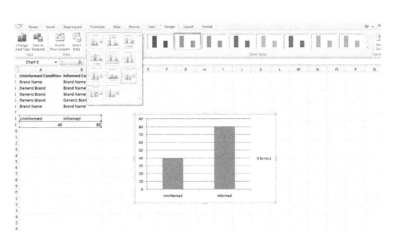

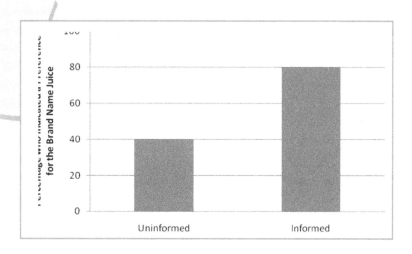

The Chart Title should be removed by clicking on it and hitting Delete. The Y axis should be labeled by clicking on it, typing in a label, and pressing Enter. Since the names under the bars provide meaningful information on the X axis, the X axis label can be removed by clicking on it and pressing Delete. Finally, the Y axis scale can be changed so it ranges from 0 to 100, by right-clicking on the Y axis and selecting the Format Axis option. The adjacent graph would be appropriate to present.

Example 2

The research question in Example 2 focused on examining whether recalling a purchase made for others makes people happier than recalling a purchase made for themselves. A pretest-posttest design was used and participants were randomly assigned to one of two conditions. Participants were first given a pretest in which they had to rate their happiness on a scale ranging from 1–5 (with 1 indicating extremely unhappy and 5 indicating extremely happy). After the pretest, participants in the "Self" condition were asked to recall a purchase they recently made for themselves and then to rate their happiness again, while participants in the "Other" condition were asked to recall a purchase they recently made for someone else and then to rate their happiness again. Thus, the type of purchase recalled (for self or other) is the independent variable and the happiness rating provided at posttest (after recalling the purchase) is the dependent variable. First, you should recognize that the dependent variable was measured on an interval scale. As such, we will need to separately calculate means and standard deviations for the groups and compare the difference in the means across them.

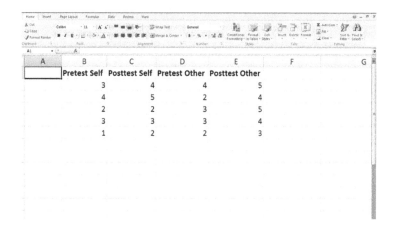

Organizing the Data in Excel

The data would need to be organized into Microsoft Excel, with separate columns for the pretest and posttest data from each group. One column could be labeled "Pretest Self" (to indicate the pretest scores from the group who recalled a purchase made for themselves), a second column could be labeled "Posttest Self" (to indicate the posttest scores from the group who recalled a purchase made for them-selves), a third column could be labeled "Pretest Other," and a fourth column could be labeled "Posttest Other." Each participant's happiness ratings would then need to be entered in the appropriate columns.

Let's assume the data shown in the figure shown on page 70 were obtained from 10 participants (with five participants in the Self condition and five in the Other condition). The figure depicts how the data should be organized.

Calculating Descriptive Statistics

Means

Since the pretest-posttest design was used for this experiment, the mean happiness pretest scores for the two groups would first need to be calculated and compared to ensure that there were no preexisting differences across the groups. If the mean pretest scores for both groups are similar, it suggests that there are no preexisting differences in happiness across the groups, and therefore that the mean posttest scores can simply be calculated and compared across groups. If the mean pretest scores for both groups are not similar, it suggests that there are preexisting differences in happiness across the groups, and mean difference scores (i.e., the difference between each participant's happiness rating at pretest and his/her happiness rating at posttest scores) would need to be calculated and compared across groups. We will consider the first scenario first.

The adjacent figure shows the pretest data from the Self condition in cells B2 to B6. To calculate the average pretest score for the Self condition, you would need to enter the formula =AVERAGE() into a blank cell and place your cursor between the empty parentheses by clicking between them. Next, you would need to place your cursor in the first cell containing data from the condition (cell B2) and then drag it down to the last cell containing data from the condition (cell B6). Finally, press Enter. Alternatively, since the cells B2:B6 contain the data, you could simply enter the formula =AVERAGE(B2:B6) into a blank cell and then press Enter.

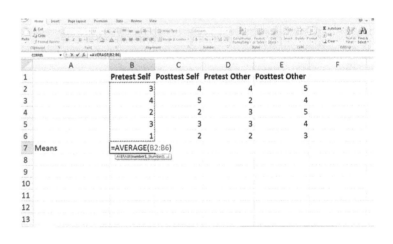

Row 7 of the adjacent figure displays the results after repeating the process for the remaining columns. The result in column B shows that the mean pretest score in the Self condition is 2.60. Column D shows that the mean pretest score in the Other condition is 2.80. Thus, it appears that the process of random assignment worked to produce equivalent groups with respect to happiness. Of primary interest, then, the results in columns C and E show that the mean posttest score in the Self condition is 3.20, while the mean posttest score in the Other condition is 4.20.

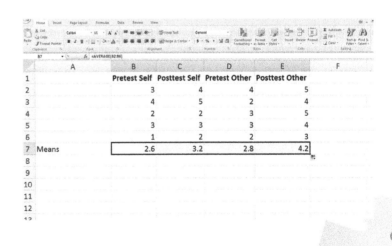

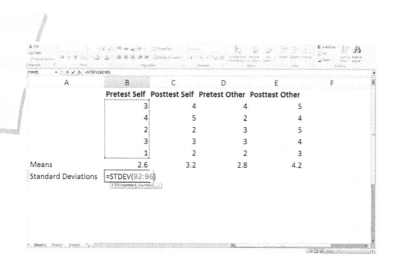

Standard Deviations

To calculate the standard deviation for the pretest scores from the Self condition, you would first need to enter the formula =STDEV() into a blank cell and place your cursor between the empty parentheses in the formula by clicking between them. Next, you would need to place your cursor in the first cell containing data from the condition (cell B2) and then drag it down to the last cell containing data from the condition (cell B6). Finally, press Enter. Alternatively, you could simply enter the formula =STDEV(B2:B6) into a blank cell and then press Enter.

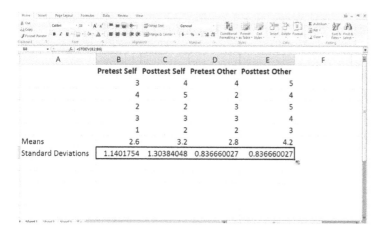

Row 8 in the adjacent figure shows the results after repeating the process for the remaining columns. The result in column B shows that the standard deviation for the pretest scores in the Self condition is 1.14 (this means that on average pretest scores in this condition are 1.14 units away from the mean). Column D shows that the standard deviation for the pretest scores in the Other condition is .84. Finally, columns C and E show that the standard deviation for the posttest scores in the Self condition is 1.30, while the standard deviation for the posttest scores in the Other condition is .84.

Since inferential statistics are beyond the scope of the labs, for our purposes we will simply observe that the mean posttest score in the Other condition is sufficiently higher than the mean posttest score in the Self condition to conclude that recalling a purchase made for someone else makes people happier than recalling a purchase made for themselves.

Graphing the Results

Before the results can be graphed, they need to be organized in two columns and two rows. Specifically, the means on the pretest would need to be entered into two columns in a single row, and the means on the posttest would need to be entered into two columns in the next row. The names of the corresponding groups/conditions would need to be placed immediately above the values of the corresponding means. The row containing the pretest means should be labeled "Pretest" and the row containing the posttest means should be labeled "Posttest." The highlighted area of the adjacent figure demonstrates how the results should be organized in Excel.

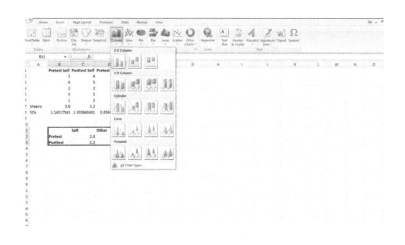

	A	B	C	D	E	F	G
1		Pretest Self	Posttest Self	Pretest Other	Posttest Other		
2		3	4	4	5		
3		4	5	2	4		
4		2	2	3	5		
5		3	3	3	4		
6		1	2	2	3		
7	Means	2.6	3.2	2.8	4.2		
8	SDs	1.1401754	1.30384048	0.836660027	0.836660027		
9							
10							
11			Self	Other			
12		Pretest	2.6	2.8			
13		Posttest	3.2	4.2			

To create the graph, you would need to highlight the group and condition names along with the means, click on the Insert tab in the toolbar, and then click on the Column option in the next toolbar that appears. As shown in the adjacent figure, several options for different types of bar graphs will be displayed. To create a clean and simple graph, you should select the first type of 2D graph (it is highlighted in the adjacent figure).

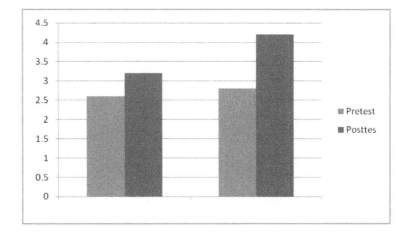

The following graph would then be created. Note that the axes are not clearly labeled and the Y axis values do not accurately reflect the scale that was used to measure happiness (a scale ranging from 1–5).

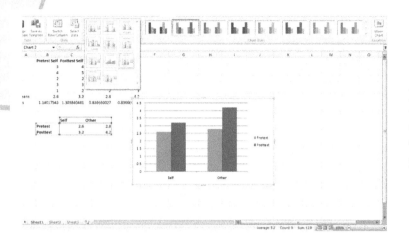

Before you can label the axes, you need to change the layout to Layout 9 using the Chart Layout option in the toolbar. This option is shown in the adjacent figure.

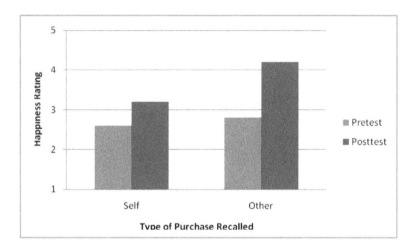

The Chart Title would then need to be removed by clicking on it and hitting Delete. The axes would need to be labeled by clicking on them, typing in a meaningful label, and pressing Enter. The scale presented on the Y axis should also be changed by right-clicking on the Y axis and selecting the Format Axis option. The adjacent graph would be appropriate to present.

Dealing with Differences in Pretest Scores

We will now consider a scenario where the pretest scores of the two groups are not equivalent. In this case, it would be inappropriate to calculate and report the mean posttest scores of the groups (because we would expect them to be different even if the manipulation of the independent variable had no effect).

	Pretest Self	Posttest Self	Pretest Other	Posttest Other		
	3	4	4	5		
	4	5	2	4		
	2	2	3	5		
	3	3	3	4		
	1	2	4	6		
Means	2.6	3.2	3.2	4.8		
SDs	1.1401754	1.30384048	0.836660027	0.836660027		

Assume that the data shown in the adjacent figure were instead obtained. For these data, the pretest scores of the two groups are not equivalent. They show that participants in the Self condition gave a mean happiness rating of 2.60, while the participants in the Other condition gave a mean happiness rating of 3.20 on the pretest.

Mean Difference Scores

When the pretest scores of the groups are not equivalent, difference scores need to be calculated. To calculate difference scores, each participant's pretest score needs to be subtracted from his/her posttest score (posttest score—pretest score = difference score). The means of the two groups' difference scores would then need to be calculated and compared. The adjacent figure shows the difference scores for each participant. Column F shows the difference scores for each participant in the Self condition, and column G shows

the difference scores for each participant in the Other condition. Row 7 of columns F and G shows the mean of these difference scores.

	A	B	C	D	E	F	G
1		Pretest Self	Posttest Self	Pretest Other	Posttest Other	Self Difference	Other Difference
2		3	4	4	5	1	1
3		4	5	2	4	1	2
4		2	2	3	5	0	2
5		3	3	3	4	0	1
6		1	2	4	6	1	2
7	Means	2.6	3.2	3.2	4.8	0.6	1.6

Standard Deviations of the Difference Scores

Rather than calculating the standard deviations of each group's pretest and posttest scores, the standard deviations of each group's difference scores would need to be calculated and reported. Row 8 of columns F and G in the adjacent figure shows the standard deviations of these difference scores.

We can now observe that the mean difference scores are sufficiently different to conclude that participants

	A	B	C	D	E	F	G
1		Pretest Self	Posttest Self	Pretest Other	Posttest Other	Self Difference	Other Difference
2		3	4	4	5	1	1
3		4	5	2	4	1	2
4		2	2	3	5	0	2
5		3	3	3	4	0	1
6		1	2	4	6	1	2
7	Means	2.6	3.2	3.2	4.8	0.6	1.6
8	SDs	1.1401754	1.30384048	0.836660027	0.836660027	0.547722558	0.547722558

who recalled making a purchase for others showed greater increases in happiness than those who recalled making a purchase for themselves.

Graphing the Results

When the pretest scores are not equivalent and difference scores are examined, a simple graph displaying the means of the difference scores should be produced. To graph the mean difference scores, you would need to enter the means in a single row and type the names of the corresponding groups in the cells immediately above the means. The highlighted section of the adjacent figure displays how the means should be organized.

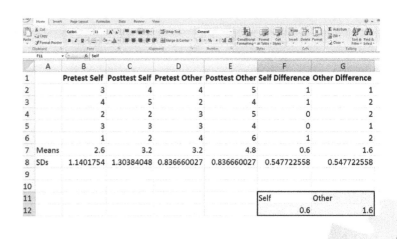

	A	B	C	D	E	F	G
1		Pretest Self	Posttest Self	Pretest Other	Posttest Other	Self Difference	Other Difference
2		3	4	4	5	1	1
3		4	5	2	4	1	2
4		2	2	3	5	0	2
5		3	3	3	4	0	1
6		1	2	4	6	1	2
7	Means	2.6	3.2	3.2	4.8	0.6	1.6
8	SDs	1.1401754	1.30384048	0.836660027	0.836660027	0.547722558	0.547722558
11						Self	Other
12						0.6	1.6

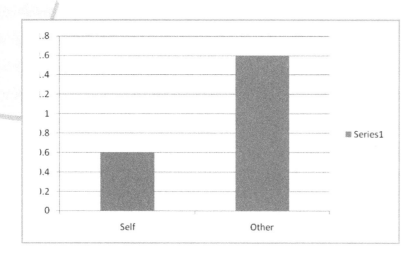

To create the graph, you would simply need to highlight the means and group names, click on the Insert tab in the toolbar, and then click on the Column option in the next toolbar. Several options for different types of bar graphs would then appear. To create a clean and simple graph, you should select the first type of 2D graph. The following graph would then be created. Note that there is no need for the Series legend and the axes are not clearly labeled.

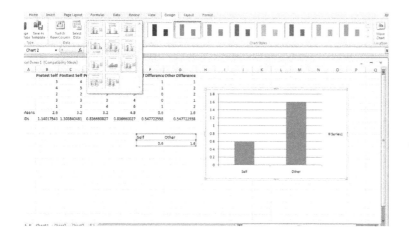

Before you can label the axes, you need to change the layout to Layout 9 using the Chart Layout option in the toolbar. This option is highlighted in the adjacent figure.

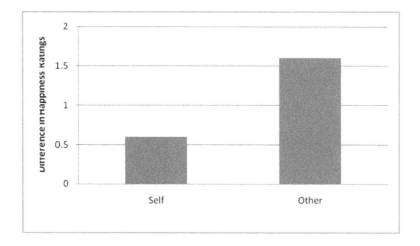

The Chart Title and Series legend should then be removed by clicking on them and hitting Delete. The axes would need to be labeled by clicking on them, typing in a meaningful label, and pressing Enter. The adjacent graph would be appropriate to present for these results.

Example 3

This example focused on examining whether priming participants with speed increases the speed they complete a simple puzzle. A posttest only design was used. Each participant completed two conditions: a "Speed" condition and a "Neutral" condition. For the Speed condition, participants read a short story about a speed racer and then completed a simple puzzle. For the Neutral condition, participants read a short story about a dog and then completed a simple puzzle. The time it took participants to complete the puzzle in each condition was measured using a concealed stopwatch. Thus, the dependent variable was measured on a ratio scale.

Organizing the Data in Excel

Before the data can be analyzed, they first need to be organized in Excel such that the data from each condition appear in separate columns. One column could be labeled "Speed" (to represent the Speed condition) and a second column could be labeled "Neutral" (to represent the Neutral condition). Assume the data (i.e., puzzle completion times in seconds) shown in the adjacent figure were obtained from five participants. Since a repeated measures design was used, each row contains the data from the same participant.

After scanning through the data, you should notice that there is an extreme score in the data set. The second subject (whose data are shown in row 3) took far longer to complete the puzzle in the Neutral condition than anyone else. The presence of this extreme score makes it less appropriate to calculate means and standard deviations because it will dramatically inflate their values in the Neutral condition. In this case, medians should be calculated and compared across the conditions. Note that an alternative way to deal with the extreme score would be to discard the data from the subject, reducing the sample to four participants and then proceeding to calculate the means and standard deviations for each condition.

Calculating Descriptive Statistics

Median

To calculate the median time in the Speed condition, you would need to enter the formula =MEDIAN() into a blank cell and then place your cursor between the empty parentheses by clicking between them. Next, you would need to place your cursor in the first cell containing data from

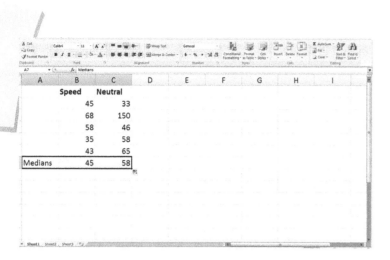

the condition (cell B2) and then drag it down to the last cell containing data from the condition (cell B6). Finally, press Enter. Note that the data do not first need to be rank ordered when Excel is used to compute the medians.

The adjacent figure shows the results after repeating this process for the remaining column (the Neutral condition). The results in row 7 show that the median time to complete the puzzle in the Speed condition is 45 seconds, while the median time to complete the puzzle in the Neutral condition is 58 seconds.

The values of the medians are sufficiently different to conclude that priming participants with a story related to speed increases the speed at which they complete a simple puzzle.

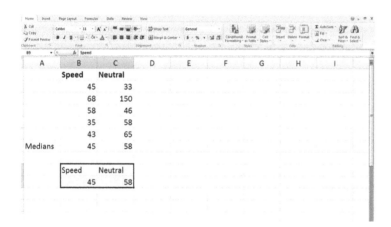

Graphing the Results

Before the results can be graphed, they need to be organized in a single row in Excel. Specifically, the medians would need to be entered into a single row with the corresponding condition names appearing immediately above the values. The highlighted area of the adjacent figure demonstrates how the results should be organized in Excel. Since the independent variable is categorical (rather than continuous) in nature, a bar graph will be most appropriate to depict these results.

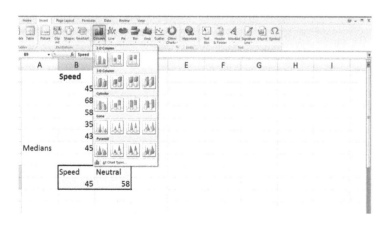

To create the bar graph, you would need to highlight the condition names and corresponding medians, click on the Insert tab in the toolbar, and then click on the Column option in the next toolbar. As shown in the adjacent figure, several options for different types of bar graphs will appear. To create a clean and simple graph, you should select the first type of 2D graph.

The following graph would then be created. Note that the axes are not clearly labeled and an unnecessary legend appears.

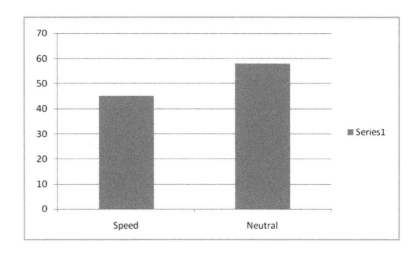

Before you can label the axes, you need to change the layout to Layout 9 using the Chart Layout option, which is depicted in the adjacent figure.

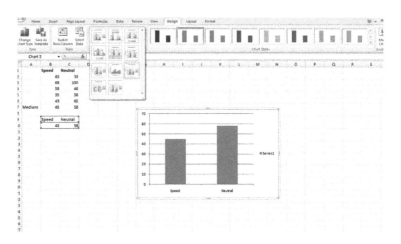

The Chart Title and Series legend should be removed by clicking on them and hitting Delete. The axes should be labeled by clicking on each, typing in a meaningful label, and pressing Enter. The adjacent graph would be appropriate to present.

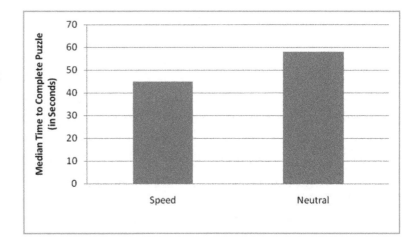

Example 4

The research question in Example 3 focused on examining the relationship between the number of friends people have on Facebook and the amount they socialize in the real (non-virtual) world. A correlational design was used. Each participant was asked to report the number of friends he/she currently has on Facebook and the number of times in the past week he/she socialized with at least one friend in a non-virtual environment. You should recognize that both of the variables were measured on a ratio scale. Since no groups were formed and nothing was manipulated, we will need to compute a correlation coefficient to describe the results.

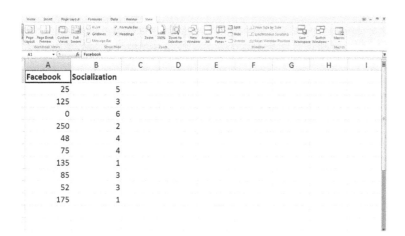

Organizing the Data in Excel

The data would first need to be organized in two columns in Excel, with one column for each variable that was measured. For this example, one column could be labeled "Facebook" and a second column could be labeled "Socialization" (to represent the amount participants reported socializing in the real world). Since correlation considers the degree to which participants' scores on one variable are related to their scores on another variable, each row must contain the same participant's data on both variables. Assume the data shown in the adjacent figure were obtained from 10 participants.

Calculating Descriptive Statistics

Correlation Coefficient

To calculate the correlation coefficient, you would need to enter the formula =CORREL() into a blank cell. You would then need to place your cursor between the empty parentheses by clicking between them. Next, you would need to place your cursor in the first cell containing data on the first variable (cell A2) and then drag it down to the last cell containing data on that variable (cell A11). Once the parentheses contain a display of (A2: A11), you would need to enter a comma (,) and then place your cursor in the first cell containing data on the second variable (cell B2) and drag it down to the last cell containing data on the second variable (cell B11). Once the parentheses contain a complete display of the ranges of cells containing the data on both

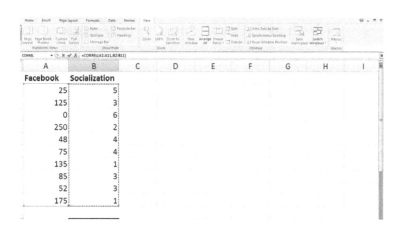

Research Methods in Psychology

variables (A2:A11,B2:B11), press Enter. The value of the correlation coefficient (-.81) will then appear.

The value of the correlation coefficient is large enough to conclude that there is a large negative relationship between the number of friends people have on Facebook and the amount they socialize in the real (non-virtual world). Specifically, as the number of Facebook friends increases, the number of socializations in the real world decreases.

Graphing the Results

Since a correlational design was used, a scatter plot is most appropriate to depict the results. To create the scatter plot, you would need to highlight the data in both columns (don't highlight the variable names), click on the Insert tab in the toolbar, and then click on the Scatter option in the next toolbar. As shown in the adjacent figure, several options for different types of graphs will appear. To create an appropriate scatter plot, you would need to select the first option.

	A	B
1	Facebook	Socialization
2	25	5
3	125	3
4	0	6
5	250	2
6	48	4
7	75	4
8	135	1
9	85	3
10	52	3
11	175	1
12		
13	Correlation	-0.80923633

The following graph would then be created. Note that the axes are not clearly labeled and an unnecessary legend appears.

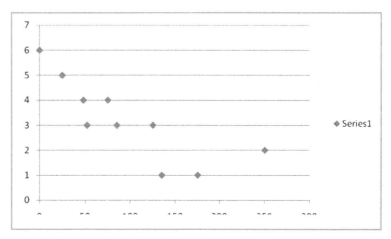

Before you can label the axes, you need to change the layout to Layout 1 using the Chart Layout option, which is depicted in the adjacent figure.

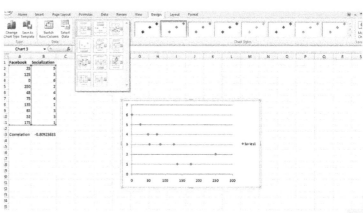

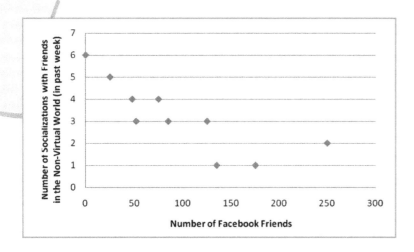

The Chart Title and Series legend should be removed by clicking on them and hitting Delete. The axes should be labeled by clicking on each, typing in a meaningful label, and pressing Enter. The adjacent graph would be appropriate to present.

CPSIA information can be obtained
at www.ICGtesting.com
Printed in the USA
LVHW05s1036290618
582147LV00003B/15/P

9 780757 579684